Emmett Dulaney

MCSE

FAST TRACK

Networking
Essentials

New
Riders

201 West 103rd Street, Indianapolis, Indiana 46290

MCSE Fast Track:
Networking Essentials

International Standard Book Number: 1-56205-939-4

Library of Congress Catalog Card Number: 98-86325

Printed in the United States of America

First Printing: September, 1998

00 99 98   4 3 2 1

Trademarks

Warning and Disclaimer

Executive Editor
Mary Foote

Acquisitions Editor
Steve Weiss

Development Editor
Nancy Warner

Managing Editor
Sarah Kearns

Project Editor
Mike La Bonne

Copy Editor
Gayle Johnson

Indexer
Chris Wilcox

Technical Editors
Andrew Brice
Grant Jones

Book Designers
Nathan Clement
Ruth Lewis

Cover Designer
Sandra Schroeder

Production
Lisa England
Carl Pierce

Contents at a Glance

TABLE OF CONTENTS

About the Author

Emmett Dulaney, MCP+I, MCSE is a consultant for D S Technical Solutions, and an instructor for a national training company. He has been teaching certification courses for the continuing education department of Indiana University/Purdue University at Fort Wayne for over four years, and is the Certification Corner columnist for *NT Systems Magazine*. In addition, Emmett is the author or co-author of over a dozen computer books, including *CNE Short Course, Sams Teach Yourself MCSE Windows NT Workstation in 14 Days*, and *MCSE TestPrep: TCP/IP*. He has also written over 100 magazine articles on computing for several publications.

About the Technical Reviewers

R. Andrew Brice currently works as a senior instructor for ProSoft I-Net Solutions in Austin, Texas. His certifications include Novell CNA and CNE, as well as the Microsoft Certified Trainer and Microsoft Certified Systems Engineer in both Windows NT 3.51 and 4.0. Since 1991, he has been providing consulting in network design and support to small and large organizations, including Fortune 1000 companies. This consulting has included training for Novell, Microsoft, and Netscape technical curricula leave, coupled with web-site development, security, and e-commerce. He specializes in the design and implementation of wide area networks (WANs). He credits his accomplishments to the love and support provided by both his wife, Susan, and his daughter, Katie. He can be reached at andrewb@flash.net.

Grant Jones has worked as a network engineer for the past five years, and is certified as an MCSE, MCP + Inet, MCT, CNE3/4 (Certified NetWare Engineer versions 3 and 4), and CNI (Certified NetWare Instructor). For the past three years, Grant has been teaching the official Microsoft core classes along with IIS and TCP/IP; he is currently working for ProSoft I-Net Solutions, where he is creating courseware for ePC certifications. Grant has written courses on Netscape Mail and IIS 4.0; the course he developed on IIS 4.0 was taught to Microsoft Visual Basic programmers in Redmond, WA. In addition, Grant has spoken at trade shows such as Internet World and Internet Commerce Expo on Internet fundamentals and electronic commerce.

DEDICATION

To Jim Scott, for showing that you CAN do what you really like. To Linda, for showing what courage really is.

ACKNOWLEDGMENTS

First and foremost, I thank Grant Jones for his conviction and belief in the product and for his patience with it, as well. I also thank Nancy Warner, the developer, Andrew Brice, Grant Jones, and Mike La Bonne, the project editor.

TELL US WHAT YOU THINK!

As the reader of this book, *you* are our most important critic and commentator. We value your opinion and want to know what we're doing right, what we could do better, what areas you'd like to see us publish in, and any other words of wisdom you're willing to pass our way.

As the Executive Editor for the Certification team at Macmillan Computer Publishing, I welcome your comments. You can fax, email, or write me directly to let me know what you did or didn't like about this book—as well as what we can do to make our books stronger.

Please note that I cannot help you with technical problems related to the topic of this book, and that due to the high volume of mail I receive, I might not be able to reply to every message.

When you write, please be sure to include this book's title and author, as well as your name and phone or fax number. I will carefully review your comments and share them with the author and editors who worked on the book.

Fax: 317-581-4663

Email: certification@mcp.com

Mail: Mary Foote
             Executive Editor
             Certification
             Macmillan Computer Publishing
             201 West 103rd Street
             Indianapolis, IN 46290 USA

Introduction

The *MCSE Fast Track* series is designed as a study aid to help you prepare for Microsoft Certification exams. The series is intended to help reinforce and clarify information that you're already familiar with. This series isn't intended to be a single source for student preparation, but rather a review of information and a set of practice materials to help increase your likelihood of success when taking the actual exam.

WHY WE DID THIS SERIES: WORDS FROM THE AUTHOR AND PUBLISHER

First, let's state this once more: New Riders *MCSE Fast Tracks* are not intended to be single sources for exam preparation. These books have been uniquely written and developed to work as supplements to your existing knowledge base.

But exactly what makes them different?

1. **Brevity.** Many other exam training materials seek Microsoft approval (you've probably seen the official "Microsoft Approved Study Guide" logo on other books, for example), meaning they must include 50% tutorial material and cover every objective for every exam in exactly the same manner, to the same degree. MCSE Fast Tracks break away from that mold by focusing on what you really need to know to pass the exams.

2. **Focus.** Fast Tracks are targeted primarily to those who know the technology but who don't yet have the certification. No superfluous information is included. *MCSE Fast Tracks* feature only what the more-experienced candidate needs to know to pass the exams. *Fast Tracks are affordable study material for the experienced professional.*

3. **Concentrated value and learning power.** Frankly, we wouldn't be surprised if Fast Tracks prove to appeal to a wider audience than just advanced-level candidates. We've tried to pack as much distilled

exam knowledge as possible into *Fast Tracks,* creating a "digest" of exam-critical information. No matter what level you're at, you may well see this digest on certification training as a logical starting point for exam study.

4. **Classroom-tested, instructor-proven.** With tens of thousands of new certification candidates entering the training routine each year, trainers like Emmett Dulaney—on the forefront of the certification education lines—are finding themselves in front of classes comprised of increased numbers of candidates with the following:

   ♦ Already a measurable base of understanding of the technology

   ♦ A desire for efficient, "just-the-facts" training

Emmett and New Riders pooled their thoughts and found that no books *truly* existed that adequately fill the following need:

To provide an easy way to review the key elements of each certification technology without being bogged down with elementary-level information, and to present this information in the light of an insider's perspective.

Emmett developed his instructional style and content to help this ever-increasing group of nonbeginners, and they in turn helped him focus the material even more. He then worked with New Riders to develop this classroom-tested material into a refined, efficient, self-instruction tool. What you see in this book is the result of that interaction.

Think of *Fast Tracks* as the set of instructor's notes you always wanted to get your hands on. These notes truly help you only if you already know the material and are ready to take on the exam itself. It's then that this book is designed to help you shine. Good luck and may your hard work pay off.

WHO SHOULD READ THIS BOOK

This book is specifically intended to help you prepare for Microsoft's Networking Essentials (70-058) exam—one of the core requirements in the MCSE program.

PART I: WHAT THE NETWORKING ESSENTIALS EXAM (70-058) COVERS

The Networking Essentials certification exam measures your ability to implement, administer, and troubleshoot computer systems in a large, processing-intensive environment. It focuses on determining your skill in four major categories:

- Standards and Terminology
- Planning
- Implementation
- Troubleshooting

The Networking Essentials certification exam uses these categories to measure your abilities. Before taking the exam, you should be proficient in the job skills discussed in the following pages.

STANDARDS AND TERMINOLOGY

The Standards and Terminology section is designed to make sure that you understand the terms and requirements of a network.

Objectives for Standards and Terminology

- Define common networking terms for LANs and WANs.
- Compare a file-and-print server with an application server.
- Compare user-level security with access permission assigned to a shared directory on a server.
- Compare a client/server network with a peer-to-peer network.
- Compare the implications of using connection-related communications with connectionless communications.
- Distinguish whether SLIP or PPP is used as the communications protocol in various situations.

- Define the communication devices that communicate at each level of the OSI model.

- Describe the characteristics and purpose of the media used in IEEE 802.3 and IEEE 802.5 standards.

- Explain the purpose of NDIS and Novell ODI network standards.

PLANNING

The Planning part of the Networking Essentials exam tests you on virtually every physical and topological component of the network.

Objectives for Planning

- Select the appropriate medium for various situations. Media choices include the following:

  - Twisted-pair cable

  - Coaxial cable

  - Fiber-optic cable

  - Wireless

- Situational elements include the following:

  - Cost

  - Distance limitations

  - Number of nodes

- Select the appropriate technology for various token-ring and Ethernet networks.

- Select the appropriate network and transport protocol or protocols for various token-ring and Ethernet networks. Protocol choices include the following:

  - DLC

  - AppleTalk

- IPX
- TCP/IP
- NFS
- SMB

◆ Select the appropriate connectivity devices for various token-ring and Ethernet networks. Connectivity devices include the following:

- Repeaters
- Bridges
- Routers
- Brouters
- Gateways

◆ List the characteristics, requirements, and appropriate situations for WAN connection services. WAN connection services include the following:

- X.25
- ISDN
- Frame relay
- ATM

IMPLEMENTATION

The Implementation component concentrates on daily administration issues and requires some knowledge of Microsoft products.

Objectives for Implementation

◆ Choose an administrative plan to meet specified needs, including performance management, account management, and security.

◆ Choose a disaster recovery plan for various situations.

- Given the manufacturer's documentation for the network adapter, install, configure, and resolve hardware conflicts for multiple network adapters in a token-ring or Ethernet network.

- Implement a NetBIOS naming scheme for all computers on a given network.

- Select the appropriate hardware and software tools to monitor trends in the network.

TROUBLESHOOTING

The Troubleshooting component of the certification exam has four components that run the entire gamut of troubleshooting.

Objectives for Troubleshooting

- Identify common errors associated with components required for communications.

- Diagnose and resolve common connectivity problems with cards, cables, and related hardware.

- Resolve broadcast storms.

- Identify and resolve network performance problems.

HARDWARE AND SOFTWARE RECOMMENDED FOR PREPARATION

The *Fast Track* series is meant to help you review concepts with which you already have training and hands-on experience. To make the most of the review, you need to have as much background and experience as possible. The best way to do this is to combine studying with working on real networks using the products you will be tested on. This section describes the minimum computer requirements you will need to build a solid practice environment.

Computers

The minimum computer requirements to ensure that you can study for everything you'll be tested on are one or more workstations running Windows 95 or NT Workstation, and two or more servers running Windows NT Server, all connected by a network.

Workstations: Windows 95 and Windows NT

- A computer that is on the Microsoft Hardware Compatibility list
- A 486DX 33 MHz
- 16 MB of RAM
- A 200 MB hard disk
- A 3 1/2-inch 1.44 MB floppy drive
- A VGA video adapter
- A VGA monitor
- A mouse or equivalent pointing device
- A two-speed CD-ROM drive
- A Network Interface Card (NIC)
- A presence on an existing network, or the use of a hub to create a test network
- Microsoft Windows 95 or NT Workstation 4.0

Servers: Windows NT Server

- Two computers on the Microsoft Hardware Compatibility List
- A 486DX2 66 MHz
- 32 MB of RAM
- A 340 MB hard disk
- A 3 1/2-inch 1.44 MB floppy drive
- A VGA video adapter
- A VGA monitor

- A mouse or equivalent pointing device

- A two-speed CD-ROM drive

- A Network Interface Card (NIC)

- A presence on an existing network, or the use of a hub to create a test network

- Microsoft Windows NT Server 4.0

OBJECTIVE REVIEW NOTES

The Objective Review Notes feature of the *Fast Track* series contains a separate section—two to a page—for each subobjective covered in the book. Each subobjective section falls under the main exam objective category, just as you'd expect to find it. It is strongly suggested that you review each subobjective and immediately make note of your knowledge level; then return to the Objective Review Notes section repeatedly and document your progress. Your ultimate goal should be to be able to review only this section and know if you are ready for the exam.

Suggested use:

1. Read the objective. Refer to the part of the book where it's covered. Then ask yourself the following questions:

    - Do you already know this material? Then check "Got it" and make a note of the date.

    - Do you need some brushing up on the objective area? Check "Review it" and make a note of the date. While you're at it, write down the page numbers you just checked, because you'll need to return to that section.

    - Is this material something you're largely unfamiliar with? Check the "Help!" box and write down the date. Now you can get to work.

2. You get the idea. Keep working through the material in this book and in the other study material you probably have. The more you get the material, the quicker you can update and upgrade each objective notes section from "Help!" to "Review it" to "Got it."

3. Cross-reference the materials YOU are using. Most people who take certification exams use more than one resource at a time. Write down the page numbers of where this material is covered in other books you're using, or which software program and file this material is covered on, or which video tape (and counter number) it's on, or whatever you need that works for you.

Think of this as your personal study diary—your documentation of how you beat this exam.

PART II: ROUNDING OUT YOUR EXAM PREPARATION

Part II of this book is designed to round out your exam preparation by providing you with the following chapters:

- "Fast Facts Review" is a digest of all "What Is Important to Know" sections from all Part I chapters. Use this chapter to review just before you take the exam: It's all here, in an easily reviewable format.

- "Insider's Spin on Exam 70-058" grounds you in the particulars for preparing mentally for this examination and for Microsoft testing in general.

- "Sample Test Questions" provides a full-length practice exam that tests you on the actual material covered in Part I. If you mastered the material there, you should be able to pass with flying colors here.

- "Hotlist of Exam-Critical Concepts" is your resource for cross-checking your tech terms. Although you're probably up to speed on most of this material already, double-check yourself anytime you run across an item you're not 100 percent certain about; it could make a difference at exam time.

- "Did You Know?" is the last-day-of-class bonus chapter: A brief touching-upon of peripheral information designed to help people using this technology to the point that they want to be certified in its mastery.

What's Important to Know About Exam 70-058

MCSE Fast Track: Networking Essentials is written as a study aid for people preparing for Microsoft Certification Exam 70-058. The book is intended to help reinforce and clarify information with which the student is already familiar. This series is not intended to be a single source for exam preparation, but rather a review of information and set of practice tests to help increase the likelihood of success when taking the actual exam.

Part I of this book is designed to help you make the most of your study time by presenting concise summaries of information that you need to understand to succeed on the exam. Each chapter covers a specific exam objective area as outlined by Microsoft:

1 **Standards and Terminology**

2 **Planning**

3 **Implementation**

4 **Troubleshooting**

ABOUT THE EXAM

Exam Number	**70-058**
Minutes	**75***
Questions	**58***
Passing Score	**793***
Single-Answer Questions	Yes
Multiple Answer with Correct Number Given	Yes
Multiple Answer Without Correct Number Given	Yes
Ranking Order	No
Choices of A-D	Yes
Choices of A-E	Very Few
Objective Categories	4

*Note: These exam criteria will no longer apply when this exam goes to an adaptive format.

▶ Define common networking terms for LANs and WANs.

▶ Compare user-level security to access permission assigned to a shared directory on a server.

▶ Compare a client/server network to a peer-to-peer network.

▶ Compare a file-and-print server to an application server.

▶ Define the communication devices that communicate at each level of the OSI model.

▶ Compare the implications of using connection-related communications to connectionless communications.

▶ Distinguish whether SLIP or PPP is used as the communications protocol for various situations.

▶ Describe the characteristics and purpose of the media used in IEEE 802.3 and IEEE 802.5 standards.

▶ Explain the purpose of NDIS and Novell ODI network standards.

CHAPTER 1

Standards and Terminology

NETWORKING BASICS

In this chapter, we'll look at the components of a network.

A *network* is a group of two or more computer systems sharing services and interacting in some manner. In most cases, this interaction is accomplished through a shared communications link, with the shared components being data. Put simply, a network is a collection of machines that have been linked both physically and through software components to facilitate communication and the sharing of information.

A *physical pathway,* known as the *transmission medium,* connects the systems, and a set of rules determines how they communicate. These rules are known as *protocols.* A network protocol is software installed on a machine that determines the agreed-upon set of rules for two or more machines to communicate with each other. One common metaphor used to describe different protocols is to compare them to human languages.

Think of a group of people in the same room who know nothing about each other. In order for them to communicate, this group must determine what language to speak, how to handle identifying each other, whether to make general announcements or have private conversations, and so on. Machines using different protocols is equivalent to one person's speaking French and another person's speaking Spanish. Machines that have different protocols installed can't communicate with each other.

Common protocols in the Microsoft family include the following:

- NetBEUI (NetBIOS Extended User Interface)
- NWLink (the NDIS-compliant version of Novell's IPX/SPX)
- DLC (Data Link Control)
- AFP (AppleTalk File Protocol)
- TCP/IP (Transmission Control Protocol/Internet Protocol)

LANs and WANs

The network can be divided into geographical areas and will fall into one of two major categories:

- Local Area Networks (LANs)
- Wide Area Networks (WANs)

A LAN is generally confined to a specific location, such as a floor, building, or some other small area. By being confined, it is possible in most cases to use only one transmission medium (cabling). The technology is less expensive to implement than in a WAN, because you are keeping all of your expenses to a small area, and generally you can obtain higher speeds of transfer.

Two outgrowths of LANs are CANs (Campus Area Networks) and MANs (Metropolitan Area Networks). In the former, the geographical location is confined to a set of buildings that constitute a campus—such as a university or corporate headquarters spanning multiple buildings. A MAN, on the other hand, is a network running throughout a metropolitan area, such as a backbone for a phone service carrier.

A WAN is as big as you care to make it. It implies multiple connected LANs that can be separated by any geographical distance. A LAN at the corporate headquarters in Indianapolis can be connected to a LAN at a field office in Chicago and to another field-office LAN in St. Louis to form a single Wide Area Network. With the unlimited geographical area, it stands to reason that the cost to implement a WAN is higher, there are more possible errors due to the distance the data must travel, and the links are typically slower than in a LAN.

Whether a LAN or WAN, the overall goals of a network are to establish a means of sharing data, to provide services, to allow for administration and security, and to reduce equipment costs. Three models, or methods of organization, are available for networking; those will be examined next.

ORGANIZATIONAL MODELS

At A Glance: Organizational Models

Centralized	All processing is done at one location
Distributed	Independent operation and local tasks
Collaborative/Cooperative	Computers cooperate and share the load to complete processing

Centralized computing was the first method of networking implemented. As the name implies, all networking is done at one central location. The best example of this would be a Unix host with a number of dumb terminals running from it. The dumb terminals are nothing more than input/output interfaces into the host, and all processing actually takes place at the host. Because all interaction is at one location, all the terminals connect directly to the host and never connect to each other.

With distributed computing, the dumb terminals are replaced by PCs. The PCs can function separately and also interact with servers. Tasks are run locally, and data is exchanged, but without the server's performing any direction. A good example of this setup would be an NT Server acting as a file server with a number of Windows 98 clients networked to it. The Windows 98 clients are capable of independent operations. When they need to perform a task involving a file, they obtain it from the server and perform the operation they need. The server gives them the file but doesn't tell them what to do with it. It is the client that determines what to do with the data that was requested.

Collaborative computing, also known as cooperative computing, enables computers to not only share resources (such as files) but also share processing. There are two methods by which this can be invoked: A server might borrow an entire processor from an idle machine to perform an action, or the server might share part of the processing with a client.

A classic example of this environment is Microsoft SQL Server. When a client requests data, SQL Server does some of the processing and sends the data to the client for the completion of the processing on that system. In all cases, the software must be written to take advantage of the environment; collaborative computing can't take place in the absence of such software.

NETWORKING MODELS

At A Glance: Networking Models

Peer-to-Peer	Cheap to implement, minimal security
Server-based	Requires a dedicated server and good security

Two types of networks can be established: peer-to-peer and server-based. We will examine these two types in the following sections.

Peer-to-Peer

In a peer-to-peer network, you take the machines currently in existence, install networking cards in them, and connect them through some type of cabling. Each machine is known as a peer and can participate in the sharing of files or resources. No server is required, so there is no additional cost for a dedicated machine, but there is also no real security.

Peer-to-peer networks require an operating system (or add-on) that can understand networking and function in this way. Microsoft's Windows 95, Windows 98, Windows NT Server, and Windows NT Workstation can all function in a peer-to-peer environment.

If file and print sharing has been enabled on a Windows 95 system, for example, you can create a share by selecting a folder and choosing to share it. By default, no password is associated with it, but you can choose to assign one that a user must know in order to access the resource. Access permissions can be Read-Only, Full, or Depends on Password. This is known as *share-level security:* Access is gained when a user supplies the correct password to access the share.

The Universal Naming Convention allows a computer name and share name (typically limited to 15 characters or less) to be used to identify a resource without tying up a drive-letter assignment. The syntax is

```
\\computername\sharename\path\file
```

If mapping is used, a redirector maps network names used by an application to a physical network device name.

Peer-to-peer networking works in small environments. If you grow beyond approximately 10 machines, the administrative overhead of establishing the shares, coupled with the lack of tight security, creates a nightmare.

Server-Based

In the presence of a server, be it NetWare or NT, you can implement *user-level security* on your network. With user-level security, permissions are based on how the user logged on and was authenticated by the server. Every user has an *account*. In this environment, you can assign permissions to shares based on user permissions or group permissions. In short, you must have a server on the network in order to have user-level security, but you can have share-level security with or without a server.

Also known as *client/server* networks, server-based networking's downside is that it requires a dedicated machine (the server); the upside is that you gain centralized administration and authentication. With centralized administration, you can add all users at one location, control logon scripts and backups, and so on. With centralized authentication, you can identify a user to your entire network based on his logon name and password, not based on each share he attempts to access.

Peer-to-peer networks can exist comfortably within server-based networks. In many businesses, combinations of the two models are used. A server-based network is used to provide e-mail and other resources to all users, and peer-to-peer networks are established within divisions to share resources among select users.

Microsoft also calls peer-to-peer networks *workgroups* and server-based networks *domains*. These terms are used interchangeably in almost all Microsoft documentation.

DIFFERENT SERVER TYPES

At A Glance: Server Types

File and Print	Holds files for client access and/or routes print jobs
Application	Applications are run on the server, and results are sent to the client

A *server* is a machine that provides resources, and every machine accessing those resources is known as a *client*. There are different types of servers. The three most common are file, print, and application servers.

File servers store files on the network for clients to access. In so doing, they provide a central location where a number of users can find the same data. They also provide a central point for backup operations, and they simplify the implementation of fault tolerance (you apply fault tolerance to the server rather than to every client, and the data is kept safe).

Print servers, as the name implies, offer printing services to clients. A single print server offers access to one or more printers to any number of clients. Microsoft uses the term *file and print server* generically to mean any server that offers file services, print services, or both.

An application server can run all or some of an application for a client. Not only does it hold data in the file server, but also it has the application needed to process that data. After all or some of the processing is complete at the server, the results are downloaded to the client.

To compare the three, the file and print servers offer a storage location for the clients. They therefore benefit greatly from large hard drives. Although RAM is important, the processor is not so important. An application server, on the other hand, requires a fast processor to run the application and get the results to the client. RAM is also important to the application server, while the size of the hard drive usually is not (within reason).

THE OSI MODEL

At A Glance: OSI Mnemonic

Layer	Mnemonic
Application	All
Presentation	People
Session	Seem
Transport	To
Network	Need
Data Link	Data
Physical	Processing

To remember the layers in reverse order, use this mnemonic: Please Do Not Throw Sausage Pizza Away.

At A Glance: Layer Purposes

Layer	Purpose
Application	Interface to network services
Presentation	Translates between Application and all others; redirector; encryption; compression
Session	Establishes rules for communication; determines synchronization
Transport	Handles network transmissions
Network	Addressing; traffic; switching
Data Link	Error checking; manages link control; communicates with cards
Physical	Network Interface Card; wire; and so on

The OSI model divides networking tasks into seven fundamentally different layers to make it easier for the industry to move forward and evolve. With the tasks segregated into functional units, a person writing the code for a network card doesn't have to worry about which applications will be run over it. Conversely, a programmer writing an application doesn't have to worry about who manufactured the network card. However, to make this work, everything must be written to comply with the boundary specifications between each of the model's seven layers.

The Physical Layer

The first layer is the Physical layer. It uses bits and signals to communicate. This is the only layer that is truly connected to the network in the sense that it is the only layer concerned with how to interpret the voltage on the wire—the 1s and 0s. This layer is responsible for understanding the electrical rules associated with devices and for determining what kind of medium is actually being used (cables, connectors, and other mechanical distinctions).

It is important to note that while the OSI model doesn't define the media used, the Physical layer is concerned with all aspects of transmitting and receiving bits on the network. Key attributes of the physical network include the following:

- The physical structure of the network

- Electrical and mechanical specifications for using the medium

- Bit transmission encoding and timing

It is also equally important to note that although the OSI model doesn't define the medium that must be used, it does define requirements that the medium must meet; and Physical layer specifications differ, depending on the physical medium. Ethernet for UTP, for example, has different Physical layer specifications than Ethernet for coax.

All network connections consist of two types of building blocks:

- **Multipoint connections** let one device communicate with two or more devices. All the devices attached using a multipoint connection share the same network transmission medium.

- **Point-to-point connections** let one device communicate with one other device. When two devices are connected through a point-to-point link, they have exclusive use of the link's data capacity.

Larger networks can be constructed by adding point-to-point links. In this case, devices rely on other devices to relay their messages. Point-to-point links can even come full circle to form a ring, allowing messages to be passed from any device to any other device on the ring.

The Data Link Layer

The second layer is the Data Link layer. It is responsible for the creation and interpretation of different frame types based on the actual physical network being used. For instance, Ethernet and token-ring networks support different and numerous frame types, and the Data Link layer must understand the difference between them.

This layer is also responsible for interpreting what it receives from the Physical layer, using low-level error detection and correction algorithms to determine when information needs to be re-sent. Network protocols, including the TCP/IP protocol suite, don't define physical standards at the physical or Data Link layer, but instead are written to make use of any standards that may currently be in use.

The boundary layer between the Data Link layer and the Network layer defines a group of agreed-upon standards for how protocols communicate and gain access to these lower layers. As long as a network protocol is appropriately written to this boundary layer, the protocols should be able to access the network, regardless of what media type is being used.

To restate at the risk of redundancy, while the OSI Physical layer is concerned with moving messages at the machine level, network communication is more involved than moving bits from one device to another. In fact, dozens of steps must be performed to transport a message from one device to another.

Real messages consist not of single bits but of meaningful groups of bits. The Data Link layer receives messages called *frames* from upper layers. A primary function of the Data Link layer is to disassemble these frames into bits for transmission and then to reconstruct frames from bits that are received.

The Data Link layer has other functions as well (although not all functions might be performed by a given network protocol stack). This layer performs the following tasks:

- ◆ Identifies devices on the network

- ◆ Controls (and possibly corrects) errors

- ◆ Controls access to the network medium

- ◆ Defines the logical topology of the network

- ◆ Controls data flow

NOTE

The Data Link layer is traditionally divided into two sublayers:

- ◆ **Logical link control (LLC).** This sublayer establishes and maintains links between communicating devices.

• **Media access control (MAC).** This sublayer controls the means by which multiple devices share the same media channel. There are several methods of performing this operation. The most popular are contention, token passing, and polling. Table 1.1 summarizes the benefits and considerations of each.

TABLE 1.1

ACCESS CONTROL METHODS

Access Control Method	Advantages	Considerations
Contention	Simple software.	Access is probabilistic (not guaranteed).
	Once access is gained, a device has complete control of the medium.	No priority mechanism.
		Collisions increase geometrically with demand.
Token passing	Each device is guaranteed media access (deterministic).	More complex software and hardware.
	Priorities might be assigned.	Might require a central control device.
	Collisions are eliminated.	
	High throughput under a heavy load.	
Polling	Each device is guaranteed media access (deterministic).	Polling uses a significant portion of network bandwidth.
	Priorities might be assigned.	Polling requires bandwidth overhead, even for devices that have nothing to transmit.
	Collisions are eliminated.	

The Network Layer

The third layer of the OSI model is the Network layer. It is mostly associated with the movement of data by means of addressing and routing. It directs the flow of data from a source to a destination, despite the fact that the machines might not be connected to the same physical wire or segment, by finding a path or route from one machine to another. If necessary, this layer can break data into smaller chunks for transmission. This is sometimes necessary when transferring data from one type of physical network to another, such as token-ring (which supports larger frame sizes) to Ethernet (which supports smaller frame sizes). Of course, the Network layer is also responsible for reassembling those smaller chunks into the original data after the data has reached its destination. For example, a number of protocols from the TCP/IP protocol suite exist in this layer, but the network protocol that is responsible for the routing and delivery of packets is the IP protocol.

To restate: The Network layer involves communication with devices on logically separate networks connected to form internetworks. Because internetworks can be large and can be constructed of different types of networks, the Network layer utilizes routing algorithms that can be used to guide packets from their source to their destination networks.

A key element of the Network layer is that each network in the internetwork is assigned a network address that can be used to route packets. The nature of those addresses and how they're used to route packets constitute the topics of addressing and switching.

Addressing

Addressing is best exemplified in TCP/IP. The most fundamental element of the Internet Protocol is the address space that IP uses. Each machine on a network is given a unique 32-bit address called an Internet address or IP address. Addresses are divided into five categories, called classes. There are currently A, B, C, D, and E classes of addresses. The unique address given to a machine is derived from the class A, B, or C addresses. Class D addresses are used for combining machines into one functional group, and Class E addresses are considered experimental and are not currently available. For now, the most important concept to understand is that each machine requires a unique address and that IP is responsible for maintaining, utilizing, and manipulating it to provide communication between two machines. The whole concept behind uniquely identifying machines is to be able to send data to one machine and one machine only, even in the event that the IP stack has to broadcast at the Physical layer.

If IP receives data from the network interface layer that is addressed to another machine or is not a broadcast, its directions are to silently discard the packet and to not continue processing it.

IP receives information in the form of packets from the Transport layer, from either TCP or UDP, and sends out data in what are commonly referred to as *datagrams*. The size of a datagram depends on the type of network that is being used, such as token ring or Ethernet. If a packet has too much data to be transmitted in one datagram, it is broken into pieces and transmitted through several datagrams. Each of these datagrams then has to be reassembled by TCP or UDP.

Switching

Switching is a vast improvement over routing that allows multiple paths to be used to deliver data. This decreases the amount of time necessary for delivery and provides redundancy in paths. Three types of switching technologies are currently employed:

- Circuit

- Message

- Packet

Circuit Switching

Circuit switching establishes a path that remains fixed for the duration of the connection. It's similar to telephone switching equipment. In the telephone world, switching equipment establishes a route between your telephone in the Midwest and a telephone in New York and maintains that connection for the duration of your call. The next time you call, the same path may or may not be used.

The advantages of circuit switching include the use of dedicated paths and a well-defined bandwidth. The disadvantages include the establishment of each connection (which can be time-consuming) and the inability of other traffic to share the dedicated media path. The latter can lead to inefficiently utilized bandwidth. Due to the need to have excess (or rather a surplus of) bandwidth, this technology tends to be expensive when compared to other options.

Message Switching

Message switching treats each message as an independent entity and is not concerned with what came before or will come after. Each message carries its own address information and details of its destination. The information is used at each switch to transfer the message to the next switch in the route. Message switches are programmed with information concerning other switches in the network that can be used to forward messages to their destinations. They can also be programmed with information about which of the routes is the most efficient, and they can send different messages through the network to the same destination via different routes (and routers).

In message switching, the complete message is sent from one switch to the next, and the whole message is stored there before being forwarded. Because the switches hold what is coming in and wait until it is all there before sending anything out, they are often called store-and-forward networks. Common uses of this technology include e-mail, calendaring, and groupware applications.

The advantages of message switching are that it can use relatively low-cost devices, data channels are shared among communicating devices, priorities can be assigned to manage traffic, and bandwidth is used rather efficiently. The disadvantage is that it is completely unacceptable for real-time applications.

Packet Switching

When most administrators think of adding switches to their network, they think of packet switches. Here, messages are divided into smaller packets, each containing source and destination address information. They can be routed through the internetwork independently. Packet size is restricted to the point where the entire packet can remain in the memory of the switching devices, and there is no need to temporarily store the data anywhere. For this reason, packet switching routes the data through the network much more rapidly and efficiently than is possible with message switching.

There are many types of packet switches. The most common are datagram and virtual circuit. With datagram packet switching, each switch node decides which network segment should be used for the next step in the packet's route. This lets switches bypass busy segments and take other steps to speed packets through the internetwork—making datagram packet switching ideally suited for LANs.

Virtual circuit packet switching establishes a formal connection between two devices and negotiates communication parameters such as the maximum message size, communication window, network path, and so on, thus creating a virtual circuit that remains in effect until the devices stop communicating. When a virtual circuit is present on a temporary basis, you'll hear the buzzword switched virtual circuit (SVC). When the virtual circuit is present for an undetermined amount of time, the buzzword used is permanent virtual circuit (PVC).

The most popular implementation of packet switching is ATM (Asynchronous Transfer Mode), which uses fixed-length 53-byte packets (which ATM advocates call cells) and sends them across the internetwork. Because the size of 53 bytes is standard, the process of negotiating packet size with each connection is eliminated, thus allowing for an increase in transfer speed.

Regardless of the technology employed, packet-switching advantages include the capability to optimize the use of bandwidth and to let many devices route packets through the same network channels. At any time, a switch may be routing packets to several different destination devices, adjusting the routes as required to get the best efficiency possible. The only disadvantage is the initial cost of the equipment, which can be sizeable.

The Transport Layer

The fourth layer is the Transport layer. It is primarily responsible for guaranteeing delivery of packets transmitted by the Network layer, although it doesn't always have to do so. Depending on the protocol being used, delivery of packets may or may not be guaranteed. When the Transport layer is responsible for guaranteeing the delivery of packets, it does so through various means of error control, including verification of sequence numbers for packets and other protocol-dependent mechanisms.

TCP/IP has two protocols at this layer of the model: Transmission Control Protocol (TCP) and User Datagram Protocol (UDP). UDP may be used for nonguaranteed delivery of packets (as well as datagrams and segments), and TCP may be used to guarantee the delivery of packets.

The Session Layer

The fifth layer is the Session layer. It is responsible for managing connections between two machines during the course of communication between them. This layer determines whether it has received all pertinent information for the session and whether it can stop receiving or transmitting data packets. This layer also has built-in error correction and recovery methods.

The Presentation Layer

The sixth layer is the Presentation layer. It is primarily concerned with the conversion of data formats, in the form of packets, from one machine to another. One common example is the sending of data from a machine that uses the ASCII format for characters to a machine that uses the EBCDIC format for characters, typically IBM mainframes.

The Presentation layer is responsible for picking up differences such as these and translating them to compatible formats. Both EBCDIC and ASCII are standards for translating characters to hexadecimal code. Letters, numbers, and symbols in one format must be translated when communicating with machines using a different format. This is the responsibility of the Presentation layer.

The Application Layer

The seventh and last layer of the OSI model is the Application layer. It acts as the arbiter or translator between users' applications and the network. Applications that want to utilize the network to transfer messages must be written to conform to networking APIs supported by the machine's networking components, such as Windows Sockets and

NetBIOS. After the application makes an API call, the Application layer determines which machine it wants to communicate with, whether a session should be set up between the communicating machines, and whether the delivery of packets needs to be guaranteed.

The Layer Relationship

At A Glance: Data Types

Layer	Data Type
Application	Message
Presentation	Packet
Session	Packet
Transport	Datagram and segment (and packet)
Network	Datagram (and packet)
Data Link	Frame
Physical	Bits and signals

Between each layer is a common boundary layer. For instance, between the Network layer and the Transport layer is a boundary that both must be able to support. It is through these boundary layers that one layer of the networking model communicates and shares valuable and necessary information with the layer above or below it. In fact, each time a layer passes data to the layer below, it adds information to it. Each time a layer receives data, it strips off its own information and passes the rest up the protocol stack.

One of the most common and useful analogies used to describe the networking model is to imagine the process a letter goes through to get to its destination.

Messages sent from one computer to another move in the same manner. Messages from one layer are packaged and placed into the next layer. Each step of the process has little to do with the preceding or following step. The kind of envelope used has nothing to do with whether you wrote the message in English, French, or German, and it certainly doesn't matter what the message was. In the same way, where you actually address the envelope—to California, Florida, or Hawaii—has absolutely nothing to do with what kind of envelope you use. The only common link between the address and the message is the envelope itself.

Lastly, it doesn't matter which vehicle—boat, plane, or train—the postal service uses to deliver the envelope to its destination address, as long as it gets there. Each layer depends on the other layers, but each layer is only mildly related to the others in terms of functionality.

Communication Devices and the OSI Model

At A Glance: Communication Devices

OSI Layer	Physical Device
Application	Gateway
Presentation	Gateway
Session	Gateway
Transport	Gateway
Network	Router
Data Link	Bridge
Physical	Repeater

A number of physical devices can be placed on a network to increase the size of the network or expand its reaches. The most common ones—and the ones that you must know for the exam—are repeaters, bridges, routers, and gateways.

Repeaters

When an electrical signal is sent across a medium, it fades along the distance (known as *attenuation*) as a result of resistance from the medium itself. Naturally, the longer the distance that is traveled, the more the signal fades. Eventually, the signal fades to a point where the receiving station can't recognize the original message (or has trouble doing so).

A *repeater* operates at the Physical layer of the OSI model and takes a signal from one LAN and sends it to another LAN—reconditioning and retiming it in the process. The reconditioning usually amplifies and boosts the signal's power level. If the signal has traveled a distance, is weak, and so on, the amplification can also be done on noise received. Therefore, most repeaters contain some method of reconditioning that subtracts electrical noise from the signal.

The repeater has no knowledge of the meaning of the individual bits in the packet. A repeater can't be addressed individually; no address field exists in the packet for a repeater.

The repeater's job is simple: It detects the signal, amplifies and retimes it, and sends it through all the ports except the one on which the signal was seen. In the case of Ethernet, the signals transmitted include data packets and even collisions. The segments of the LAN that are connected participate in the media access mechanism, such as CSMA/CD or token. Because it works only at the lower level, a repeater can't be used to connect different segments of different topologies, but it *can* be used to connect segments of the same topology with different media.

It is important to note that since the repeater has no real knowledge of the data it is carrying, no error-checking is performed. Therefore, any errors (such as CRC) are passed from one segment to the next without any ability to stop it.

On the positive side, by not performing any filtering, the repeater is transparent to protocols and doesn't slow down the network's performance perceptibly.

NOTE

Most often, repeaters are discussed, and thought of, as devices that retransmit signals down a wire. However, repeaters can also be wireless and used to extend the range of a microwave signal.

Repeater pros and cons are summarized in Table 1.2.

TABLE 1.2

PROS AND CONS OF REPEATERS

Pros	Cons
Allow you to extend the network over large distances	Have no knowledge of addressing or data types
Do not affect the speed of the network	Can't ease network congestion problems
Can connect network segments of different media	Limit the number of repeaters that can be used

Bridges

Bridges connect two separate networks to form a logical one by operating at the Data Link layer of the OSI model. Bridges rely on MAC addresses for their operation. Unlike repeaters, bridges examine the packet's destination address before forwarding it to other segments.

Bridges isolate the media access mechanisms of the LANs to which they are connected. If a packet has a destination address on the same network segment as the source of the signal, the bridge ignores the signal. If the destination address is different from the source address network segment, the bridge sends the message along in a fashion similar to what a repeater would. Since bridges are selective about which data packets can be transferred, they are useful in solving traffic bottlenecks. It must be noted, however, that bridges do not reduce traffic caused by broadcast packets or broadcast storms.

> **NOTE** Bridges check the destination address against addresses that they know to be on the same network as the source. If the address is not known to be on the same segment, the bridge forwards the signal. This is an important concept, and worth repeating: The bridge doesn't know that the address is elsewhere. It only knows that it isn't here, so it sends it on.

Although they are effective for a small number of LANs, bridges lose many of their benefits as the number of LANs grows. Bridges only operate at the Data Link layer, and the best source routing information (needed for decisions about routes through the network) is a component of the Network layer.

Bridge pros and cons are summarized in Table 1.3.

TABLE 1.3

PROS AND CONS OF BRIDGES

Pros	Cons
Can act as a repeater and extend distance	Slower than repeaters due to the need to examine addresses
Easy to install, load, and configure	Can't perform effective balancing on larger networks
Can restrict flow and ease congestion	More expensive than repeaters
Useful for protocols that can't be routed	Can't prevent broadcast storms
Have good cost-to-performance ratio	Certain applications might not run on bridge networks

Routers

Routers are the most complicated of the three devices thus far, operating at the Network layer of the OSI model. While bridges are limited to examining data packet MAC addresses, routers go beyond this and can examine the network address—which has routing information encoded in it. Routers can use this information to make intelligent decisions about routes and paths.

In their simplest form, routers—like bridges—can be used to connect network segments. Whereas bridges only know to forward what they don't recognize, routers are aware of multiple paths that lead to a destination address and know which path is best.

Each network segment is assigned a specific address and is then referred to as a *subnetwork* or *subnet*. Each node on the network is then assigned an address. Every data packet sent contains the destination network address and the node address. The optimum path can then be determined by looking at the internal routing table.

One of the biggest differences between bridges and routers is the ability to identify where data is going. A router must initialize and maintain the routing table and determine the next hop in the packet's journey; a router is expected to be able to identify the address and only send packets for which it has a network address. If a matching address isn't found in the routing table, the packet is discarded.

To get at the Network layer and find the information it needs, the router must first strip off the Data Link layer. After it finds the information, it repackages the data packet. A key advantage of routers comes into play during this operation: Since the data is unpacked and repacked, there is an opportunity to transform the data to the data frame needed for a particular architecture. For example, an Ethernet packet can be repackaged and sent over a token ring network by the router's unpacking the Ethernet data frame and repacking with a token ring frame.

Almost every router made today can support multiple protocols. Here are the most common (in alphabetical order):

- CLNP
- DECnet
- IPX/SPX
- PPP
- PPTP
- SLIP
- SNA
- SNAP
- TCP/IP
- X.25
- XNS Protocols

While this list is impressive, there are some noticeable absences, because some protocols can't be routed:

- DLC
- LAT
- NetBEUI

Router pros and cons are summarized in Table 1.4.

TABLE 1.4

PROS AND CONS OF ROUTERS

Pros	Cons
Can perform more functions than bridges	Considerably more difficult to install than bridges
Can interconnect network segments of differing architectures	More expensive than repeaters or bridges
Can manage load balancing and sharing	Work only with routable protocols
Can be used to control broadcast storms	Static routing can cause problems
Can choose the best path and make dynamic changes	Much slower than bridges or repeaters due to additional functions

More on Routing Tables

An important concept to remember is that bridges that maintain tables keep track of hardware addresses for the segments they are connected to. Routers maintain routing tables (which can be global or local) that refer to network addresses. To make it more clear, bridges know the addresses of actual machines they are connected to (and transfer data for addresses not found in their tables). Routers don't know actual machine addresses. Instead, they know the addresses of other networks and the routers that handle packets going into those networks.

Global routing tables are pretty much a thing of the past. With global routing tables, there is an entry for every node on the network in every table. This information is invaluable for determining the best path. However, it's impossible to maintain with a large network.

With local routing, routing tables are much smaller, because each router maintains information pertinent to the *local* portion of the internetwork that they are connected to.

The tables—whether global or local—can be static or dynamic. With static routing, someone (usually the administrator) must manually place every entry in the routing table. Each router must always use the same route to send data—even if it doesn't represent the best route. The biggest drawback of this—aside from all the time required in keeping the tables updated—is that if there is no route to a network address, the packet can't be sent to the receiver.

With dynamic routing, routers exchange packets that contain routing information, and the routing tables are updated automatically. In order to keep the tables as current as possible, an individual router broadcasts information whenever it detects a change in the network. *Discovery* is used to find information about possible routes. If two or more routes are available for sending data, dynamic routers can choose the best route. Picking the best route is based on one of two algorithms:

- **Distance-vector algorithm**, wherein the best possible path is the shortest path (which could also turn out to be the most expensive). Most routers use a simplifying metric called a hop metric to measure distances in terms of hops. The number of hops is a measure of the number of times a packet must be processed by a router before it reaches its destination. RIP (Routing Information Protocol) would be an example of this type of algorithm used by TCP/IP.

- **Link-state algorithm**, which calculates the best route to use based on network traffic, connection speed, and other costs. OSPF (Open Shortest Path First) is an example of a link-state algorithm used by TCP/IP.

NOTE   When discussing protocols such as RIP, it is important to note that blanket statements can never be issued, because there are quite often multiple versions of the same thing. As an example, one of the biggest problems with RIP routers is that they can't pass along information about subnet values, such as masks and lengths. RIP II routers, however, do support and pass along information about subnets, including mask values and variable lengths. Most older routers support only RIP, while newer ones support RIP and RIP II.

ICMP (Internet Control Message Protocol) is included as a part of every TCP/IP implementation and is enabled automatically. ICMP can add routes to your routing tables even if dynamic routing isn't enabled.

Defined in RFCs 792 and 1256, ICMP uses a simple router-discovery method of asking neighboring routers to identify themselves. It then takes that information (only for routers directly attached to the network) and checks or adds entries to the routing table.

Brouters

Bridges perform limited functions but can work with all protocols. Routers, on the other hand, perform more-complex functions but can work with only certain protocols. Brouters come into play as a combination of the best features of the two.

If a routable packet is received, the brouter routes the data to the appropriate destination. If a nonroutable protocol sends data, however, the brouter bridges the data based on the hardware address. In order to perform both functions, the brouter must contain both a routing table and a bridging table. As common sense would dictate, in order to do so, brouters must operate at both the Network and Data Link layers of the OSI model.

More expensive and complex than either bridges or routers, brouters can be invaluable in solving an internetworking problem if you must connect your Unix (TCP/IP) network to LAN Manager or NT (running NetBEUI). If you are not in a position where you need to worry about multiple protocols consisting of routable and nonroutable, it would be better to go with a router or bridge than with a brouter.

Gateways

Gateways are often lumped into discussions about bridging and routing, when in fact the service they perform is similar but different by one major factor: With a gateway, data is translated between two different data formats or network architectures.

A classic example is converting e-mail from the native network protocol to SMTP—Simple Mail Transport Protocol. Another common use is to connect LANs to mainframes that use SNA. SNA doesn't use the same address scheme as most LANs, so you must fool the mainframe network into thinking that the LAN devices are on the mainframe.

Gateways perform much higher-level translations that any other component and thus work at the Application layer of the OSI model.

When packets arrive at a gateway, all the information is stripped off the data until it reaches the layer where it can translate the information. It then repacks the information using the format needed for the destination.

NOTE

There are many different types of gateways, all involving some type of data translation. Depending on the type of translation taking place, the gateway may operate at an OSI layer lower than Application. A few work at the Session layer, and a handful touch the Network layer. The vast majority, however, function at the Application layer.

Gateway pros and cons are summarized in Table 1.5.

TABLE 1.5

PROS AND CONS OF GATEWAYS

Pros	Cons
Can connect completely different systems	More expensive than other devices
Specialize in one task only	Difficult to install and configure. Depending on the level of translation, can be very slow.

CONNECTION-ORIENTED COMMUNICATIONS

There are two methods by which communication can occur at the network—connection-oriented and connectionless. With connection-related communication, error correction and flow control are provided at internal nodes along the path of the message. Neither error correction nor flow control is provided by internal nodes in a connectionless state.

To use an analogy, assume that you want to communicate with another person. There are two basic kinds of communication: phone and mail. When communicating on the phone, you know right away if the other person hears you or not, because it is a one-to-one communication (TCP). When you mail someone a letter, you never know if he got it or not. You only know there is a problem if someone tells you that the letter was lost (if the recipient tells you he never got it, the post office calls and says it was destroyed, and so on). The mail example represents UDP.

Most networks use some combination of both. In TCP/IP, for example, TCP is a connection-oriented protocol. It has a counterpart, UDP, that performs the exact same functions as TCP, only in a connectionless state. The advantage of connectionless communication is that data can be processed and moved more quickly because the internal nodes only forward and don't have to track connections, worry about flow, or provide retransmission.

SLIP AND PPP

Line protocols are used for phone-based connections and connecting to the Internet. In most Microsoft Windows operating systems, including NT Workstation, NT Server, Windows 95, and Windows 98, support is included for two different line protocols: SLIP and PPP. PPTP, an extension of PPP, is also available.

Serial Line Internet Protocol (SLIP)

SLIP is an industry standard that supports TCP/IP connections made over serial lines. Unfortunately, SLIP has several limitations:

- It supports only TCP/IP. It doesn't support IPX or NetBEUI.
- It requires static IP addresses. It doesn't support DHCP.
- It transmits authentication passwords as clear text. It doesn't support encryption.
- It usually requires a scripting system for the logon process.

Most Windows operating systems support SLIP client functionality only; operation as a SLIP server is not supported.

Point-to-Point Protocol (PPP)

The limitations of SLIP prompted the development of a newer industry-standard protocol, Point-to-Point Protocol (PPP). Some of the advantages of PPP include the following:

- It supports TCP/IP, IPX, NetBEUI, and others.
- It supports DHCP or static addresses.
- It supports encryption for authentication.
- It doesn't require a scripting system for the logon process.

New to Windows NT is support for PPP multilink, which lets you combine multiple physical links into one logical connection. A client with two ordinary phone lines and two 28.8 Kbps modems, for example, could establish a PPP multilink session with a RAS server that has an effective throughput of up to 57.6 Kbps. The two modems don't have to be the same type or speed. Both the RAS server and the DUN client must have PPP multilink enabled.

Point-to-Point Tunneling Protocol (PPTP)

New to many of the Windows operating systems is an extension to PPP called Point-to-Point Tunneling Protocol (PPTP). It lets clients connect to remote servers over the Internet.

PPTP lets a DUN client establish a communications session with a RAS server over the Internet. PPTP enables multiprotocol virtual private networks (VPNs) so that remote users can gain secure encrypted access to their corporate networks over the Internet. Because PPTP encapsulates TCP/IP, NWLink, and NetBEUI, it allows the Internet to be used as a backbone for NWLink and NetBEUI.

To use PPTP, first establish a connection from the DUN client to the Internet, and then establish a connection to the RAS server over the Internet.

> **NOTE** You can also select which of the network transport protocols (TCP/IP, IPX, or NetBEUI) you want to use after you have made a connection to the remote network.

802 STANDARDS

At A Glance: 802 Standards

802.1	Internetworking
802.2	Logical Link Control
802.3	Carrier Sense with Multiple Access and Collision Detection (CSMA/CD)
802.4	Token Bus LAN
802.5	Token Ring LAN
802.6	Metropolitan Area Network (MAN)
802.7	Broadband Technical Advisory Group
802.8	Fiber Optic Technical Advisory Group
802.9	Integrated Voice/Data Networks
802.10	Network Security
802.11	Wireless Networks
802.12	Demand Priority Access LAN, 100BaseVG AnyLAN

The IEEE (Institute of Electrical and Electronic Engineers) is the largest professional organization in the world. The 802 subcommittee of that organization has developed a series of standards for networking. The IEEE standards govern lower-layer protocols and interactions with transmission media. Recognized and reissued by the ISO, they are also known as the ISO 802 standards.

IEEE 802.1

The IEEE 802.1 standard defines internetworking.

IEEE 802.2

The IEEE 802.2 standard defines an LLC sublayer that is used by other lower-layer protocols. Because these lower-layer protocols can use a single LLC protocol layer, Network layer protocols can be designed independently of both the network's Physical layer and MAC sublayer implementations.

The LLC appends to packets a header that identifies the upper-layer protocols associated with the frame. This header also declares the processes that are the source and destination of each packet.

IEEE 802.3

The IEEE 802.3 standard defines a network derived from the Ethernet network originally developed by Digital, Intel, and Xerox. This standard defines characteristics related to the MAC sublayer of the Data Link layer and the OSI Physical layer. With one minor distinction—frame type—IEEE 802.3 Ethernet functions identically to DIX Ethernet v.2. These two standards can even coexist on the same cabling system, although devices using one standard can't communicate directly with devices using the other.

The MAC sublayer uses a type of contention access called *Carrier Sense with Multiple Access and Collision Detection* (*CSMA/CD*). This technique reduces the incidence of collision by having each device listen to the network to determine if it's quiet ("carrier sensing"); a device attempts to transmit only when the network is quiescent. This reduces but doesn't eliminate collisions, because signals take some time to propagate through the network. As devices transmit, they continue to listen so that they can detect a collision should it occur. When a collision occurs, all devices cease transmitting and send a "jamming" signal that notifies all stations of the collision. Then, each device waits a random amount of time before attempting to transmit again. This combination of safeguards significantly reduces collisions on all but the busiest networks.

IEEE 802.4

The 802.4 standard describes a network with a bus physical topology that controls media access with a token mechanism. This standard was designed to meet the needs of industrial automation systems but has gained little popularity. Both baseband and broadband (using 75 ohm coaxial cable) configurations are available.

IEEE 802.5

The IEEE 802.5 standard was derived from IBM's token ring network, which employs a ring logical topology and token-based media-access control. Data rates of 1, 4, and 16 Mbps have been defined for this standard.

IEEE 802.6

The IEEE 802.6 standard describes a MAN standard called *Distributed Queue Dual Bus* (*DQDB*). Much more than a data network technology, DQDB is suited to data, voice, and video transmissions.

The network is based on fiber-optic cable in a dual-bus topology, and traffic on each bus is unidirectional. When operated in pairs, the two buses provide a fault-tolerant configuration.

Bandwidth is allocated using time slots, and both synchronous and asynchronous modes are supported.

IEEE 802.7

The IEEE 802.7 standard represents the Broadband Technical Advisory Group.

IEEE 802.8

The IEEE 802.8 standard represents the Fiber Optic Technical Advisory Group.

IEEE 802.9

The IEEE 802.9 standard supports a 10 Mbps asynchronous channel, along with 96 64 Kbps (6 Mbps total bandwidth) of channels that can be dedicated to specific data streams. The total bandwidth is 16 Mbps. This standard is called Isochronous Ethernet (IsoEnet) and is designed for settings that have a mix of "bursty" and time-critical traffic.

IEEE 802.10

IEEE 802.10 is a standard for network security.

IEEE 802.11

IEEE 802.11 is a standard for wireless LANs and is currently under development. A CSMA/CD method has been approved, but the final standard is pending.

IEEE 802.12

The IEEE 802.12 standard is based on a 100 Mbps proposal promoted by AT&T, IBM, and Hewlett-Packard. Called 100VG-AnyLAN, the network is based on a star-wiring topology and a contention-based access method whereby devices signal the wiring hub when they need to transmit data. Devices can transmit only when granted permission to by the hub. This standard is intended to provide a high-speed network that can operate in mixed Ethernet and token ring environments by supporting both frame types.

IEEE 802.3 and IEEE 802.5 Media

IEEE 802.2 (topology-independent), IEEE 802.3 (based on Ethernet), and IEEE 802.5 (based on token ring) are the most commonly used IEEE 802 standards. The IEEE 802.3 Physical layer definition describes signaling methods (both baseband and broadband), data rates, media, and topologies.

Several Physical layer variants also have been defined. Each variant is named following a convention that states the signaling rate (1 or 10) in Mbps, baseband (BASE) or broadband (BROAD) mode, and a designation of the media characteristics.

The following list details the IEEE 802.3 variants:

- **1BASE5.** This 1 Mbps network utilizes UTP cable with a signal range up to 500 meters (250 meters per segment). A star physical topology is used.

- **10BASE5.** Typically called Thick Ethernet, or Thicknet, this variant uses a large-diameter (10 mm) "thick" coaxial cable with a 50-ohm impedance. A data rate of 10 Mbps is supported with a signaling range of 500 meters per cable segment on a physical bus topology.

- **10BASE2.** Similar to Thicknet, this variant uses a thinner coaxial cable that can support cable runs of 185 meters. (In this case, the "2" indicates an approximate cable range that is really 185 meters.) The transmission rate remains at 10 Mbps, and the physical topology is a bus. This variant typically is called Thin Ethernet, or Thinnet.

- **10BASE-F.** This variant uses fiber-optic cables to support 10 Mbps signaling with a range of 4 kilometers. Three subcategories include 10BASE-FL (fiber link), 10BASE-FB (fiber backbone), and 10BASE-FP (fiber passive).

- **10BROAD36.** This broadband standard supports channel signal rates of 10 Mbps. A 75-ohm coaxial cable supports cable runs of 1,800 meters (up to 3,600 meters in a dual-cable configuration) using a physical bus topology.

- **10BASE-T.** This variant uses UTP cable in a star physical topology. The signaling rate remains at 10 Mbps, and devices can be up to 100 meters from a wiring hub.

- **100BASE-X.** This proposed standard is similar to 10BASE-T but supports 100 Mbps data rates.

The IEEE 802.5 standard doesn't describe a cabling system. Most implementations are based on the IBM cabling system, which uses twisted-pair cable wired in a physical star.

NDIS AND ODI

The Network Driver Interface Specification (NDIS), a standard developed by Microsoft and 3Com Corp., describes the interface between the network transport protocol and the Data Link layer network adapter driver. The following list details the goals of NDIS:

- To provide a vendor-neutral boundary between the protocol and the network adapter driver so that any NDIS-compliant protocol stack can operate with any NDIS-compliant adapter driver.

- To define a method for binding multiple protocols to a single driver so that the adapter can simultaneously support communications under multiple protocols. In addition, this method lets you bind one protocol to more than one adapter.

The Open Data Link Interface (ODI), developed by Apple and Novell, serves the same function as NDIS. Originally, ODI was written for NetWare and Macintosh environments. Like NDIS, ODI provides rules that establish a vendor-neutral interface between the protocol stack and the adapter driver. This interface also allows one or more network drivers to support one or more protocol stacks.

WHAT IS IMPORTANT TO KNOW

The following list summarizes the chapter and accentuates the key concepts to memorize for the exam:

- A transmission medium is a physical pathway that connects systems.

- Protocols are rules for network communication.

- Share-level security is based on the resource you want to share. It is the only type of security available without a server.

- User-level security requires a server to authenticate users. It bases what the user can do on the network on that person's authentication.

- An account is required for every user on a server-based network and is identified by the user's name and password.

- Commit to memory the OSI model. Use the mnemonic All People Seem To Need Data Processing to memorize the order of the layers.

- Headers are added to the message as it travels down the layers, and they are stripped from the message as it travels up the layers.

- Brouters operate at both the Data Link and Network layers. They perform the functions of a bridge and a router.

- Most protocols are routable, so it is easier to remember those that are not: NetBEUI, DLC, and LAT (a DEC protocol).

OBJECTIVES

▶ Select the appropriate media for various situations. Media choices include the following:
- Twisted-pair cable
- Coaxial cable
- Fiber-optic cable
- Wireless

▶ Situational elements include the following:
- Cost
- Distance limitations
- Number of nodes

▶ Select the appropriate technology for various token-ring and Ethernet networks.

▶ Select the appropriate network and transport protocol(s) for various token-ring and Ethernet networks. Protocol choices include the following:
- DLC
- AppleTalk
- IPX
- TCP/IP
- NFS
- SMB

▶ continues...

CHAPTER *2*

Planning

OBJECTIVES continued

▶ Select the appropriate connectivity devices for various token-ring and Ethernet networks. Connectivity devices include the following:
  · Repeaters
  · Bridge
  · Routers
  · Brouters
  · Gateways

▶ List the characteristics, requirements, and appropriate situations for WAN connection services. These include the following:
  · X.25
  · ISDN
  · Frame Relay
  · ATM

TRANSMISSION MEDIA

At A Glance: Transmission Media

Cable	Cost	Installation	Capacity	Range	EMI
Thinnet	Less than STP and more than UTP	Easy	Typically 10MBps	185 meters	Less sensitive than UTP
Thicknet	More than STP and less than fiber	Not as easy as Thinnet	Typically 10MBps	500 meters	Less sensitive than UTP
Shielded Twisted-Pair (STP)	More than UTP and less than Thicknet	Relatively easy	From 16MBps to 500MBps	100 meters	Less sensitive than UTP
Unshielded Twisted-Pair (UTP)	Cheapest	Easy	10MBps to 100MBps	100 meters	Most sensitive of all
Fiber Optic	Most expensive	Hard	Typically 100MBps	Kilometers	Least sensitive of all

Transmission media make possible the transmission of the electronic signals from one computer to another. These electronic signals express data values in the form of binary (on/off) impulses. The signals are transmitted through the network using a combination of electronic devices (such as network boards and hubs) and transmission media (such as cables and radio) until they reach the desired destination computer.

All signals transmitted between computers consist of some form of electromagnetic (EM) waveform, ranging from radio frequencies through microwave transmissions and infrared light. Different media are used to transmit the signals, depending on the frequency of the EM waveform. Figure 2.1 illustrates the range of electromagnetic waveforms (known as the electromagnetic spectrum) and their associated frequencies.

Radio frequency waves are often used for LAN signaling. Radio frequencies can be transmitted across electrical cables (twisted-pair or coaxial) or by using radio broadcast transmission.

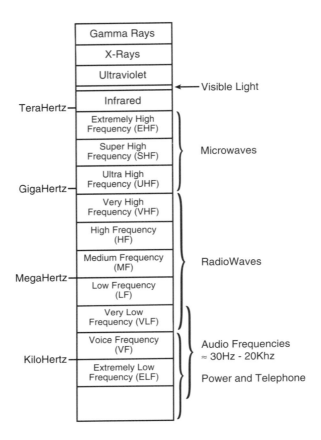

FIGURE 2.1
The electromagnetic spectrum.

Microwave transmissions can be used for tightly focused transmissions between two points. Microwaves are used to communicate between Earth stations and satellites, for example, and they are also used for line-of-sight transmissions on the earth's surface. In addition, microwaves can be used in low-power forms to broadcast signals from a transmitter to many receivers. Cellular phone networks are examples of systems that use low-power microwave signals to broadcast signals.

Infrared light is ideal for many types of network communications. It can be transmitted across relatively short distances and can be either beamed between two points or broadcast from one point to many receivers. Infrared and higher frequencies of light also can be transmitted through fiber-optic cables. The next sections examine examples of network transmission media and describe the advantages and disadvantages of each media type.

Characteristics of Transmission Media

Each type of transmission media has special characteristics that make it suitable for a specific type of service. The following sections focus on bandwidth, attenuation, and electromagnetic interference.

Bandwidth

In computer networking, the term *bandwidth* refers to the measure of the capacity of a medium to transmit data. A medium that has a high capacity, for example, has a high bandwidth, whereas a medium that has limited capacity has a low bandwidth. Bandwidth can be best understood by comparing it to a hose. If a half-inch garden hose can carry water from a trickle up to two gallons per minute, that hose can be said to have a bandwidth of two gallons per minute. A four-inch fire hose, however, might have a bandwidth that exceeds 100 gallons per minute.

Data transmission rates frequently are stated in terms of the bits that can be transmitted per second. An Ethernet LAN theoretically can transmit 10 million bits per second and has a bandwidth of 10 megabits per second (Mbps).

The bandwidth that a cable can accommodate is determined in part by the cable's length. A short cable generally can accommodate greater bandwidth than a long cable, which is one reason why all cable designs specify maximum lengths for cable runs. Beyond those limits, the highest-frequency signals can deteriorate, and errors begin to occur in data signals.

The two ways to allocate the capacity of transmission media are with baseband and broadband transmissions. Baseband devotes the entire capacity of the medium to one communication channel. Broadband lets two or more communication channels share the bandwidth of the communications medium. Baseband is the most common mode of operation. Most LANs function in baseband mode, for example. Baseband signaling can be accomplished with both analog and digital signals.

Although you might not realize it, you have a great deal of experience with broadband transmissions. Consider, for example, that the TV cable coming into your house from an antenna or a cable provider is a broadband medium. Many television signals can share the bandwidth of the cable because each signal is modulated using a separately assigned frequency. You can use the television tuner to choose the channel you want to watch by selecting its frequency. This technique of dividing bandwidth into frequency bands is called *frequency-division multiplexing* (FDM) and works only with analog signals. Another technique, called *time-division multiplexing* (TDM), supports digital signals.

Figure 2.2 shows the difference between baseband and broadband modes of operation.

Multiplexing

Multiplexing is a technique that allows broadband media to support multiple data channels. Multiplexing makes sense under a number of circumstances:

- When media bandwidth is costly. A high-speed leased line, such as a T1 or T3, is expensive to lease. If the leased line has sufficient bandwidth, multiplexing can allow the same line to carry mainframe, LAN, voice, videoconferencing, and various other data types.

- When bandwidth is idle. Many organizations have installed fiberoptic cable that is used to only partial capacity. With the proper equipment, a single fiber can support hundreds of megabits—or even a gigabit or more—of data.

- When large amounts of data must be transmitted through lowcapacity channels. Multiplexing techniques can divide the original data stream into several lower-bandwidth channels, each of which can be transmitted through a lower-capacity medium. The signals can then be recombined at the receiving end.

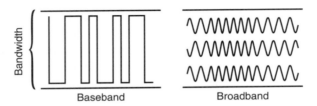

FIGURE 2.2
Baseband and broadband transmission modes.

Multiplexing refers to combining multiple data channels for transmission on a common medium. *Demultiplexing* refers to recovering the original separate channels from a multiplexed signal. Multiplexing and demultiplexing are performed by a multiplexor (also called a *mux*), which usually has both capabilities.

Frequency-Division Multiplexing

Figure 2.3 illustrates frequency-division multiplexing (FDM). This technique works by converting all data channels to analog form. Each analog signal can be modulated by a separate frequency (called a *carrier frequency*) that makes it possible to recover that signal during the demultiplexing process. At the receiving end, the demultiplexor can select the desired carrier signal and use it to extract the data signal for that channel.

FDM can be used in broadband LANs (a standard for Ethernet also exists). One advantage of FDM is that it supports bidirectional signaling on the same cable.

Time-Division Multiplexing

Time-division multiplexing (TDM) divides a channel into time slots that are allocated to the data streams to be transmitted, as shown in Figure 2.4. If the sender and receiver agree on the time-slot assignments, the receiver can easily recover and reconstruct the original data streams.

TDM transmits the multiplexed signal in baseband mode. Interestingly, this process makes it possible to multiplex a TDM multiplexed signal as one of the data channels on an FDM system. Conventional TDM equipment utilizes fixed-time divisions and allocates time to a channel, regardless of that channel's level of activity. If a channel isn't busy, its time slot isn't being fully utilized.

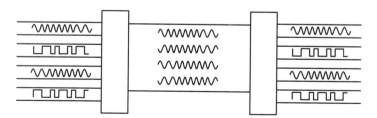

FIGURE 2.3
Frequency-division multiplexing.

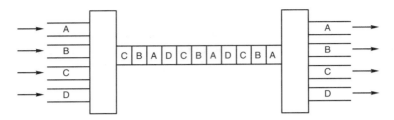

FIGURE 2.4
Frequency-division multiplexing.

Because the time divisions are programmed into the configurations of the multiplexors, this technique often is referred to as *synchronous TDM*. If using the capacity of the data medium more efficiently is important, a more sophisticated technique, *statistical time-division multiplexing* (*StatTDM*), can be used. A stat-mux uses the time slot technique but allocates time slots based on the traffic demand on the individual channels, as shown in Figure 2.5. Notice that Channel B is allocated more time slots than Channel A, and that Channel C is allocated the fewest time slots. Channel D is idle, so no slots are allocated to it. To make this procedure work, the data transmitted for each time slot includes a control field that identifies the channel to which the data in the time slot should be assigned.

Attenuation

Attenuation is a measure of how much a signal weakens as it travels through a medium. This book doesn't discuss attenuation in formal terms, but it does address the impact of attenuation on performance.

FIGURE 2.5
Statistical time-division multiplexing.

Attenuation is a contributing factor to why cable designs must specify limits in the lengths of cable runs. When signal strength falls below certain limits, the electronic equipment that receives the signal can experience difficulty isolating the original signal from the noise present in all electronic transmissions. The effect is exactly like trying to tune in distant radio signals. Even if you can lock on to the signal on your radio, the sound generally still contains more noise than the sound for a local radio station.

Electromagnetic Interference

Electromagnetic interference (EMI) consists of outside electromagnetic noise that distorts the signal in a medium. When you listen to an AM radio, for example, you often hear EMI in the form of noise caused by nearby motors or lightning. Some network media are more susceptible to EMI than others.

Crosstalk is a special kind of interference caused by adjacent wires. Crosstalk is a particularly significant problem with computer networks, because large numbers of cables are often located close together with minimal attention to exact placement.

Cable Media

For the Networking Essentials exam, you need to know how to make decisions about network transmission media based on some of the factors described in this chapter. The following sections discuss four types of network cabling media:

- ◆ Coaxial cable

- ◆ Twisted-pair cable

- ◆ Fiber-optic cable

- ◆ Wireless

Coaxial Cable

Coaxial cables were the first cable types used in LANs. As shown in Figure 2.6, coaxial cable gets its name because two conductors share a common axis. The cable is most frequently referred to as a coax.

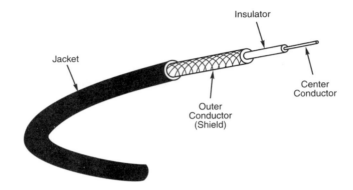

FIGURE 2.6
Four components of a coaxial cable.

The components of a coaxial cable are as follows:

- A center conductor. Although usually solid copper wire, this some-times is made of stranded wire.

- An outer conductor forms a tube surrounding the center conduc-tor. This conductor can consist of braided wires, metallic foil, or both. The outer conductor, frequently called the shield, serves as a ground and also protects the inner conductor from EMI.

- An insulation layer keeps the outer conductor spaced evenly from the inner conductor.

- A plastic encasement (jacket) protects the cable from damage.

Types of Coaxial Cable

The two basic classifications for coaxial cable are

- Thinnet

- Thicknet

Thinnet

Thinnet is a light and flexible cabling medium that is inexpensive and easy to install. Table 2.1 illustrates some Thinnet classifications. Note that Thinnet falls under the RG-58 family, which has a 50 ohm imped-ance. Thinnet is approximately .25 inches (6 mm) in thickness.

TABLE 2.1

THINNET CABLE CLASSIFICATIONS

Cable	Description	Impedance
RG-58/U	Solid copper center	50 ohm
RG-58 A/U	Wire strand center	50 ohm
RG-58 C/U	Military version of RG-58 A/U	50 ohm

Thinnet cable can reliably transmit a signal for 185 meters (about 610 feet). Although it's called 10Base2 to give the impression that it can run 200 meters, this is erroneous. It should really be called 10Base1.85.

Thicknet

Thicknet is thicker in diameter than Thinnet (approximately 0.5 inches). Because it is thicker and doesn't bend as readily as Thinnet, Thicknet cable is harder to work with. A thicker center core, however, means that Thicknet can carry more signals for a greater distance than Thinnet.

Thicknet can transmit a signal approximately 500 meters (1650 feet). Thicknet cable is sometimes called Standard Ethernet (although other cabling types described in this chapter are used for Ethernet also). Thicknet can be used to connect two or more small Thinnet LANs into a larger network.

Because of its greater size, Thicknet is also more expensive than Thinnet. Thicknet can be installed safely outside, running from building to building, such as with cable TV.

Coaxial Characteristics

You should be familiar with the installation, cost, bandwidth, and EMI resistance characteristics of coaxial cable. The following sections discuss some of the characteristics of coaxial cable.

Installation

Coaxial cable typically is installed in two configurations: daisy-chain (from device to device—Ethernet) and star (ARCnet). Both are shown in Figure 2.7.

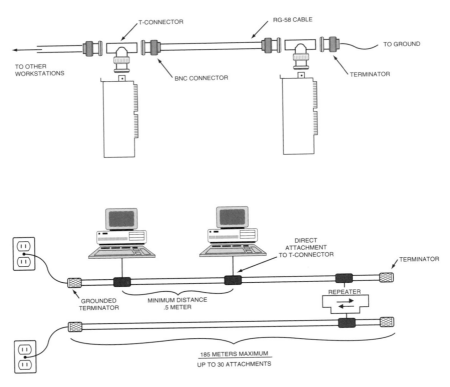

FIGURE 2.7
Coaxial wiring configurations.

The Ethernet cabling shown in the figure is an example of Thinnet, which uses RG-58-type cable. Devices connect to the cable by means of T-connectors. Cables are used to provide connections between T-connectors. One characteristic of this type of cabling is that the ends of the cable run must be terminated by a special connector, called a *terminator*. The terminator contains a resistor that is matched to the characteristics of the cable (such as a 50 ohm terminator for RG-58 cable). The resistor prevents signals that reach the end of the cable from bouncing back and causing interference.

Coaxial cable is reasonably easy to install because it is robust and difficult to damage. In addition, connectors can be installed with inexpensive tools and a bit of practice. The device-to-device cabling approach can be difficult to reconfigure, however, when new devices can't be installed near an existing cabling path.

Cost

The coaxial cable used for Thinnet falls at the low end of the cost spectrum, whereas Thicknet is among the more costly options.

Bandwidth

LANs that employ coaxial cable typically have a bandwidth between 8.5 Mbps (ARCnet) and 10 Mbps (Ethernet). Thicker coaxial cables offer higher bandwidth, and the potential bandwidth of coaxial is much higher than 10 Mbps. Current LAN technologies, however, don't take advantage of this potential.

EMI Characteristics

All copper media are sensitive to EMI, although the shield in coax makes the cable fairly resistant. Coaxial cables, however, do radiate a portion of their signal, and electronic eavesdropping equipment can detect this radiated signal.

Connectors for Coaxial Cable

Two types of connectors are commonly used with coaxial cable. The most common is the British Naval Connector (BNC), which is also called British Naval Communications. Figure 2.8 depicts the following characteristics of BNC connectors and Thinnet cabling:

- A BNC T-connector connects the network board in the PC to the network. The T-connector attaches directly to the network board.

- BNC cable connectors attach cable segments to the T-connectors.

- A BNC barrel connector connects to Thinnet cables.

- Both ends of the cable must be terminated. A BNC terminator is a special connector that includes a resistor that is carefully matched to the characteristics of the cable system.

- One of the terminators must be grounded. A wire from the connector is attached to a grounded point, such as the center screw of a grounded electrical outlet.

In contrast, Thicknet uses N-connectors, which screw on instead of using a twist lock (see Figure 2.9). As with Thinnet, both ends of the cable must be terminated, and one end must be grounded.

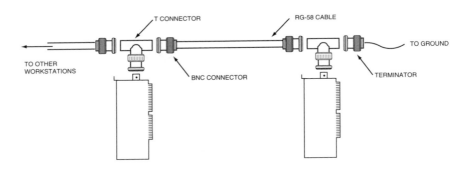

FIGURE 2.8
Thinnet uses BNC T-connectors.

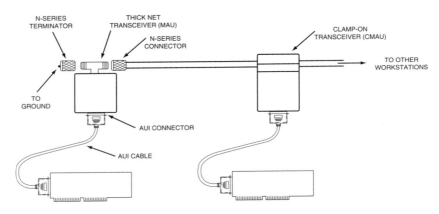

FIGURE 2.9
Thicknet connectors and cabling.

Workstations don't connect directly to the cable with Thicknet. Instead, a connecting device called a *transceiver* is attached to the Thicknet cable. This transceiver has a port for an AUI (Attachment Unit Interface) connector, and an AUI cable (also called a transceiver cable or a drop cable) connects the workstation to the Thicknet medium. Transceivers can connect to Thicknet cables in the following two ways:

+ Transceivers can connect by cutting the cable and using N-connectors and a T-connector on the transceiver. As a result, the original method is now used rather infrequently.

♦ The more common approach is to use a clamp-on transceiver, which has pins that penetrate the cable without the need for cutting it. Because clamp-on transceivers force sharp teeth into the cable, they frequently are referred to as vampire taps.

You can use a transceiver to connect a Thinnet LAN to a Thicknet backbone.

Coax and Fire Code Classifications

The space above a drop ceiling (between the ceiling and the floor of a building's next level) is extremely significant to both network administrators and fire marshals. This space (called the plenum—see Figure 2.10) is a convenient place to run network cables. The plenum is typically an open space in which air circulates freely, so fire marshals pay special attention to it.

The most common outer covering for coaxial cabling is polyvinyl chloride (PVC). PVC cabling gives off poisonous fumes when it burns. For that reason, fire codes prohibit PVC cabling in the plenum because poisonous fumes in the plenum can circulate freely throughout the building.

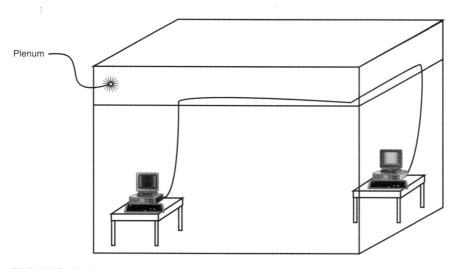

Plenum

FIGURE 2.10
The plenum between the ceiling of one level and the floor of the next.

Plenum-grade coaxial cabling is specially designed to be used without conduit in plenums, walls, and other areas where fire codes prohibit PVC cabling. Plenum-grade cabling is less flexible and more expensive than PVC cabling, so it is used primarily where PVC cabling can't be used.

Twisted-Pair

Twisted-pair cable has become the dominant cable type for all new network designs that employ copper cable. Among the several reasons for the popularity of twisted-pair cable, the most significant is its low cost. Twisted-pair cable is inexpensive to install and offers the lowest cost per foot of any cable type.

A basic twisted-pair cable consists of two strands of copper wire twisted together, as shown in Figure 2.11. This twisting reduces the sensitivity of the cable to EMI and also reduces the tendency of the cable to radiate radio frequency noise that interferes with nearby cables and electronic components. This is because the radiated signals from the twisted wires tend to cancel each other out. (Antennas, which are purposely designed to radiate radio frequency signals, consist of parallel, not twisted, wires.)

Twisting also controls the tendency of the wires in the pair to cause EMI in each other. Whenever two wires are in close proximity, the signals in each wire tend to produce noise, called *crosstalk,* in the other. Twisting the wires in the pair reduces crosstalk in much the same way that twisting reduces the tendency of the wires to radiate EMI.

Two types of twisted-pair cable are used in LANs: shielded and unshielded.

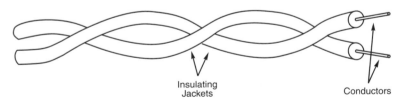

Insulating
Jackets

Conductors

FIGURE 2.11
Twisted-pair cable.

Shielded Twisted-Pair (STP) Cable

Shielded twisted-pair cabling consists of one or more twisted pairs of cables enclosed in a foil wrap and woven copper shielding. Figure 2.12 shows IBM Type 1 cabling, the first cable type used with IBM Token Ring. Early LAN designers used shielded twisted-pair cable because the shield further reduces the tendency of the cable to radiate EMI and thus reduces the cable's sensitivity to outside interference.

Coaxial and STP cables use shields for the same purpose. The shield is connected to the ground portion of the electronic device to which the cable is connected. A *ground* is a portion of the device that serves as an electrical reference point. Usually it literally is connected to a metal stake driven into the ground. A properly grounded shield prevents signals from getting into or out of the cable.

As shown in Figure 2.12, IBM Type 1 cable includes two twisted pairs of wire within a single shield. Various types of STP cable exist. Some shield each pair individually, and others shield several pairs. The engineers who design a network's cabling system choose the exact configuration. IBM designates several twisted-pair cable types to use with their Token Ring network design, and each cable type is appropriate for a given kind of installation. A completely different type of STP is the standard cable for Apple's AppleTalk network. Because so many different types of STP cable exist, stating precise characteristics is difficult. The following sections, however, offer some general guidelines.

Cost

STP cable costs more than thin coaxial or unshielded twisted-pair cable. STP is less costly, however, than thick coax or fiber-optic cable.

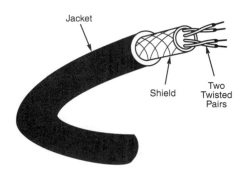

FIGURE 2.12
A shielded twisted-pair cable.

Installation

Naturally, different network types have different installation requirements. One major difference is the connector used. Apple LocalTalk connectors generally must be soldered during installation, a process that requires some practice and skill on the part of the installer. IBM Token Ring uses a unisex data connector (the connectors are both male and female) that can be installed with such common tools as a knife, a wire stripper, and a large pair of pliers.

In many cases, installation can be greatly simplified by using prewired cables. You must learn to install the required connectors, however, when your installation requires the use of bulk cable.

STP cable tends to be rather bulky. IBM Type 1 cable is approximately ½ inch (13 mm) in diameter. Therefore, it can take little time to fill up cable paths with STP cables.

Capacity

STP cable has a theoretical capacity of 500 Mbps, although few implementations exceed 155 Mbps with 100-meter cable runs. The most common data rate for STP cable is 16 Mbps, which is the top data rate for Token Ring networks.

Attenuation

All varieties of twisted-pair cable have attenuation characteristics that limit the length of cable runs to a few hundred meters, although a 100-meter limit is most common.

EMI Characteristics

The shield in STP cable results in good EMI characteristics for copper cable, comparable to the EMI characteristics of coaxial cable. This is one reason STP might be preferred to unshielded twisted-pair cable in some situations. As with all copper cables, STP is sensitive to interference and vulnerable to electronic eavesdropping.

Connectors for STP

AppleTalk and Token Ring networks can be cabled using UTP cable and RJ-45 connectors, but both networks originated as STP cabling systems. For STP cable, AppleTalk employs a DIN-type connector, shown in Figure 2.13. IBM, on the other hand, uses the IBM Data Connector, shown in Figure 2.14.

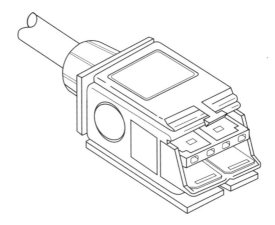

FIGURE 2.13
The connector used with STP cable.

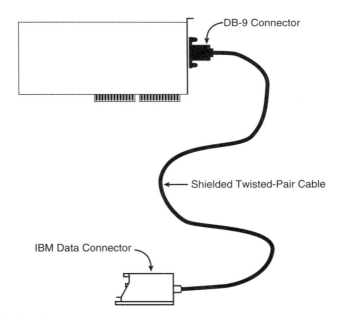

FIGURE 2.14
A PC card ready to connect to a Token Ring network.

The IBM Data Connector is unusual because it doesn't come in two gender configurations. Instead, any IBM Data Connector can be snapped to any other IBM Data Connector.

Unshielded Twisted-Pair (UTP) Cable

Unshielded twisted-pair cable doesn't incorporate a braided shield into its structure. However, the characteristics of UTP are similar in many ways to STP, differing primarily in attenuation and EMI. As shown in Figure 2.15, several twisted pairs can be bundled in a single cable. These pairs typically are color-coded to distinguish them.

Telephone systems commonly use UTP cabling. Network engineers can sometimes use existing UTP telephone cabling (if it is new enough and of a high-enough quality to support network communications) for network cabling.

UTP cable is a latecomer to high-performance LANs because engineers only recently solved the problems of managing radiated noise and susceptibility to EMI. Now, however, a clear trend toward UTP is in operation, and all new copper-based cabling schemes are based on UTP.

UTP cable is available in the following five grades, or categories:

- **Categories 1 and 2**. These voice-grade cables are suitable only for voice and for low data rates (below 4 Mbps). Category 1 was once the standard voice-grade cable for telephone systems. The growing need for data-ready cabling systems, however, has caused Categories 1 and 2 cable to be supplanted by Category 3 for new installations.

- **Category 3**. As the lowest data-grade cable, this type of cable generally is suited for data rates up to 10 Mbps. Some innovative schemes, however, let the cable support data rates up to 100 Mbps. Category 3, which uses four twisted pairs with three twists per foot, is now the standard cable used for most telephone installations.

- **Category 4**. This data-grade cable, which consists of four twisted pairs, is suitable for data rates up to 16 Mbps.

- **Category 5**. This data-grade cable, which also consists of four twisted pairs, is suitable for data rates up to 100 Mbps. Most new cabling systems for 100 Mbps data rates are designed around Category 5 cable.

UTP cable offers an excellent balance of cost and performance characteristics, as discussed in the following sections.

FIGURE 2.15
A multipair UTP cable.

Cost

UTP cable is the least costly of any cable type, although properly installed Category 5 tends to be fairly expensive. In some cases, existing cable in buildings can be used for LANs, although you should verify the category of the cable and know the length of the cable in the walls. Distance limits for voice cabling are much less stringent than for data-grade cabling.

Installation

UTP cable is easy to install. Some specialized equipment might be required, but the equipment is low in cost and can be mastered with a bit of practice. Properly designed UTP cabling systems easily can be reconfigured to meet changing requirements.

As noted earlier, however, Category 5 cable has stricter installation requirements than lower categories of UTP. Special training is recommended for dealing with Category 5 UTP.

Capacity

The data rates possible with UTP have increased from 1 Mbps, past 4 and 16 Mbps, to the point where 100 Mbps data rates are now common.

Attenuation

UTP cable shares similar attenuation characteristics with other copper cables. UTP cable runs are limited to a few hundred meters, with 100 meters as the most frequent limit.

EMI Characteristics

Because UTP cable lacks a shield, it is more sensitive to EMI than coaxial or STP cables. The latest technologies make it possible to use UTP in the vast majority of situations, provided that reasonable care is taken to avoid electrically noisy devices such as motors and fluorescent lights. Nevertheless, UTP might not be suitable for noisy environments such as factories. Crosstalk between nearby unshielded pairs limits the maximum length of cable runs.

Connectors for UTP

The most common connector used with UTP cables is the RJ-45 connector, shown in Figure 2.16. These connectors are easy to install on cables and are also extremely easy to connect and disconnect. An RJ-45 connector has eight pins and looks like a common RJ-11 telephone jack. They are slightly different sizes and won't fit together: An RJ-11 has only four pins.

Distribution racks, shelves, and patch panels are available for large UTP installations. These accessories let you organize network cabling and also provide a central spot for expansion and reconfiguration. One necessary accessory, a jack coupler, is a small device that attaches to a wall plate or a patch panel and receives an RJ-45 connection. Jack couplers can support transmission speeds of up to 100 Mbps.

Fiber-Optic Cable

In almost every way, fiber-optic cable is the ideal cable for data transmission. Not only does this type of cable accommodate extremely high bandwidths, but it also presents no problems with EMI and supports durable cables and cable runs as long as several kilometers. The two disadvantages of fiber-optic, however, are cost and difficulty of installation.

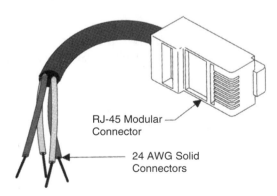

RJ-45 Modular Connector

24 AWG Solid Connectors

FIGURE 2.16
An RJ-45 connector.

The center conductor of a fiber-optic cable is a fiber that consists of highly refined glass or plastic designed to transmit light signals with little loss. A glass core supports a longer cabling distance, but a plastic core is typically easier to work with. The fiber is coated with a cladding that reflects signals back into the fiber to reduce signal loss. A plastic sheath protects the fiber. See Figure 2.17.

A fiber-optic network cable consists of two strands separately enclosed in plastic sheaths—one strand sends and the other receives. Two types of cable configurations are available: loose and tight. Loose configurations incorporate a space between the fiber sheath and the outer plastic encasement; this space is filled with a gel or other material. Tight configurations contain strength wires between the conductor and the outer plastic encasement. In both cases, the plastic encasement must supply the strength of the cable, while the gel layer or strength wires protect the delicate fiber from mechanical damage.

Optical fiber cables don't transmit electrical signals. Instead, the data signals must be converted into light signals. Light sources include lasers and light-emitting diodes (LEDs). LEDs are inexpensive but produce a fairly poor quality of light suitable for less-stringent applications. The end of the cable that receives the light signal must convert the signal back to an electrical form. Several types of solid-state components can perform this service.

One of the significant difficulties of installing fiber-optic cable arises when two cables must be joined. The small cores of the two cables (some are as small as 8.3 microns) must be lined up with extreme precision to prevent excessive signal loss.

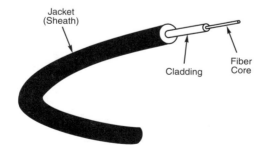

Jacket
(Sheath)

Cladding

Fiber
Core

FIGURE 2.17
A fiber-optic cable.

As with all cable types, fiber-optic cables have their share of advantages and disadvantages.

Cost

The cost of the cable and connectors has fallen significantly in recent years. However, the electronic devices required are significantly more expensive than comparable devices for copper cable. Fiber-optic cable is also the most expensive cable type to install.

Installation

Greater skill is required to install fiber-optic cable than to install most copper cables. However, improved tools and techniques have reduced the training required. Still, fiber-optic cable requires greater care, because the cables must be treated fairly gently during installation. Every cable has a minimum bend radius, for example, and fibers are damaged if the cables are bent too sharply.

It is also important not to stretch the cable during installation.

Capacity

Fiber-optic cable can support high data rates (as high as 200,000 Mbps), even with long cable runs. Although UTP cable runs are limited to less than 100 meters with 100 Mbps data rates, fiber-optic cables can transmit 100 Mbps signals for several kilometers.

Attenuation

Attenuation in fiber-optic cables is much lower than in copper cables. Fiber-optic cables can carry signals for several kilometers.

EMI Characteristics

Because fiber-optic cables don't use electrical signals to transmit data, they are totally immune to electromagnetic interference. These cables are also immune to a variety of electrical effects that must be taken into account when designing copper cabling systems.

Because the signals in fiber-optic cable are not electrical in nature, they can't be detected by the electronic eavesdropping equipment that detects electromagnetic radiation. Therefore, fiber-optic cable is the perfect choice for high-security networks.

Wireless

The extraordinary convenience of wireless communications has placed an increased emphasis on wireless networks in recent years. Technology is expanding rapidly and will continue to expand into the near future, offering more and better options for wireless networks.

Presently, you can subdivide wireless networking technology into three basic types that correspond to three basic networking scenarios:

- **Local area networks (LANs)**. Occasionally, you will see a fully wireless LAN, but more typically, one or more wireless machines will function as members of a cable-based LAN. A LAN with both wireless and cable-based components is called a *hybrid*.

- **Extended local networks**. A wireless connection serves as a backbone between two LANs. For instance, a company with office networks in two nearby but separate buildings could connect those networks using a wireless bridge.

- **Mobile computing**. A mobile machine connects to the home network using cellular or satellite technology. The following sections describe these technologies and some of the networking options available with each.

Wireless networks are especially useful in the following situations:

- Spaces where cabling would be impossible or inconvenient. These include open lobbies, inaccessible parts of buildings, older buildings, historical buildings where renovation is prohibited, and outdoor installations.

- People who move around a lot within their work environment. Network administrators, for instance, must troubleshoot a large office network. Nurses and doctors need to make rounds at a hospital.

- Temporary installations. These situations include any temporary department set up for a specific purpose that soon will be torn down or relocated.

- People who travel outside of the work environment and need instantaneous access to network resources.

Wireless Communications with LANs

It is often advantageous for a network to include some wireless nodes. Typically, though, the wireless nodes will be part of what is otherwise a traditional, cable-based network. An access point is a stationary transceiver connected to the cable-based LAN that lets the cordless PC communicate with the network. The access point acts as a conduit for the wireless PC.

The process is initiated when the wireless PC sends a signal to the access point; from there, the signal reaches the network. The truly wireless communication, therefore, is the communication from the wireless PC to the access point. An access point transceiver is one of several ways to achieve wireless networking. Some of the others are described in later sections.

You can classify wireless LAN communications according to transmission method. The four most common LAN wireless transmission methods are as follows:

- Infrared
- Laser
- Narrow-band radio
- Spread-spectrum radio

The following sections look briefly at these important wireless transmission methods.

Infrared Transmission

You use an infrared communication system every time you control your television with a remote control. The remote control transmits pulses of infrared light that carry coded instructions to a receiver on the TV. This technology can also be adapted to network communication.

There are four varieties of infrared communications:

- **Broadband optical telepoint**. This method uses broadband technology. Data transfer rates in this high-end option are competitive with those for a cable-based network.
- **Line-of-sight infrared**. Transmissions must occur over a clear line-of-sight path between transmitter and receiver.

- **Reflective infrared**. Wireless PCs transmit toward a common, central unit, which then directs communication to each of the nodes.

- **Scatter infrared**. Transmissions reflect off floors, walls, and ceilings until (theoretically) they finally reach the receiver.

Because of the imprecise trajectory, data transfer rates are slow. The maximum reliable distance is around 100 feet. Infrared transmissions typically are limited to within 100 feet. Within this range, however, infrared is relatively fast. Infrared's high bandwidth supports transmission speeds of up to 10 Mbps. Infrared devices are insensitive to radio-frequency interference, but reception can be degraded by bright light. Because transmissions are tightly focused, they are fairly immune to electronic eavesdropping.

Laser Transmission

High-powered laser transmitters can transmit data for several thousand yards when line-of-sight communication is possible. Lasers can be used in many of the same situations as microwave links (described later in this chapter), without requiring an FCC license. On a LAN scale, laser light technology is similar to infrared technology.

Narrow-Band Radio Transmission

In narrow-band radio communications (also called single-frequency radio), transmissions occur at a single radio frequency. The range of narrow-band radio is higher than infrared, effectively enabling mobile computing over a limited area. Neither the receiver nor the transmitter must be placed along a direct line of sight; the signal can bounce off walls, buildings, and even the atmosphere, but heavy walls, such as steel or concrete enclosures, can block the signal.

Spread-Spectrum Radio Transmission

Spread-spectrum radio transmission is a technique originally developed by the military to solve several communication problems. Spread-spectrum improves reliability, reduces sensitivity to interference and jamming, and is less vulnerable to eavesdropping than single-frequency radio. As its name suggests, spread-spectrum transmission uses multiple frequencies to transmit messages. Two techniques employed are *frequency hopping* and *direct sequence modulation*. Frequency hopping switches (hops) among several available frequencies (see Figure 2.18), staying on each frequency for a specified interval of time. The transmitter and receiver must remain synchronized during a process called a *hopping sequence* in order for this technique to work. Range for this type of transmission is up to two miles outdoors and 400 feet indoors. Frequency hopping typically transmits at up to 250 Kbps, although some versions can reach as high as 2 Mbps.

Direct sequence modulation breaks original messages into parts called *chips* (see Figure 2.19), which are transmitted on separate frequencies. To confuse eavesdroppers, decoy data can also be transmitted on other frequencies. The intended recipient knows which frequencies are valid and can isolate the chips and reassemble the message. Eavesdropping is difficult because the correct frequencies are not known, and the eavesdropper can't isolate the frequencies carrying true data. Because different sets of frequencies can be selected, this technique can operate in environments that support other transmission activity. Direct sequence modulation systems operating at 900 MHz support bandwidths of 2 to 6 Mbps.

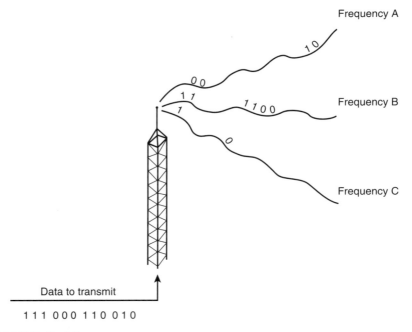

FIGURE 2.18
Frequency hopping employs various frequencies for a specific time period.

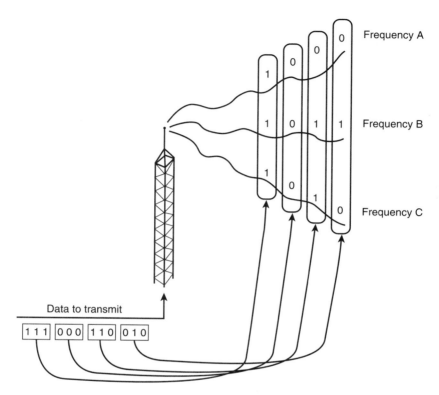

Frequency A

Frequency B

Frequency C

Data to transmit

| 1 1 1 | 0 0 0 | 1 1 0 | 0 1 0 |

FIGURE 2.19
Direct sequence modulation.

Extended LANs (Wireless Bridging)

Wireless technology can connect LANs in two different buildings into an extended LAN. Of course, this capability is also available through other technologies (such as a T1 line or a leased line from a telephone provider), but depending on the conditions, a wireless solution is sometimes more cost-effective.

A wireless bridge acts as a network bridge, merging two local LANs over a wireless connection. Wireless bridges typically use spread-spectrum radio technology to transmit data for up to three miles. (Antennas at each end of the bridge should be placed in an appropriate location, such as a rooftop.) A device called a long-range wireless bridge has a range of up to 25 miles.

Mobile Computing

Mobile computing is a growing technology that provides almost unlimited range for traveling computers by using satellite and cellular phone networks to relay the signal to a home network. Mobile computing typically is used with portable PCs or personal digital assistant (PDA) devices.

There are three forms of mobile computing:

- **Packet-radio networking**. The mobile device sends and receives network-style packets via satellite. Packets contain a source and destination address, and only the destination device can receive and read the packet.

- **Cellular networking**. The mobile device sends and receives cellular digital packet data (CDPD) using cellular phone technology and the cellular phone network. Cellular networking provides very fast communications.

- **Satellite station networking**. Satellite mobile networking stations use satellite microwave technology.

Microwave

Microwave technology has applications in all three of the wireless networking scenarios: LAN, extended LAN, and mobile networking. As shown in Figure 2.20, microwave communication can take two forms: terrestrial (ground) links and satellite links. The frequencies and technologies employed by these two forms are similar, but as you'll see, distinct differences exist between them.

Terrestrial Microwave

Terrestrial microwave communication employs Earth-based transmitters and receivers. The frequencies used are in the low-gigahertz range, which limits all communications to line-of-sight. You probably have seen terrestrial microwave equipment in the form of telephone relay towers, which are placed every few miles to relay telephone signals cross-country.

Microwave transmissions typically use a parabolic antenna that produces a narrow, highly directional signal. A similar antenna at the receiving site is sensitive to signals only within a narrow focus. Because the transmitter and receiver are highly focused, they must be adjusted carefully so that the transmitted signal is aligned with the receiver.

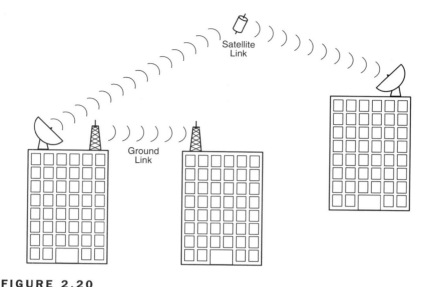

FIGURE 2.20
Terrestrial and microwave satellite links.

A microwave link frequently is used to transmit signals in instances in which it would be impractical to run cables. If you need to connect two networks separated by a public road, for example, you might find that regulations restrict you from running cables above or below the road. In such a case, a microwave link is an ideal solution.

Some LANs operate at microwave frequencies at low power and use nondirectional transmitters and receivers. Network hubs can be placed strategically throughout an organization, and workstations can be mobile or fixed. This approach is one way to enable mobile workstations in an office setting. In many cases, terrestrial microwave uses licensed frequencies. A license must be obtained from the FCC, and equipment must be installed and maintained by licensed technicians.

Terrestrial microwave systems operate in the low-gigahertz range, typically at 4 to 6 GHz and 21 to 23 GHz, and costs are highly variable depending on requirements. Long-distance microwave systems can be quite expensive but might be less costly than alternatives. (A leased telephone circuit, for example, represents a costly monthly expense.) When line-of-sight transmission is possible, a microwave link is a one-time expense that can offer greater bandwidth than a leased circuit.

Costs are decreasing for low-power microwave systems for the office. Although these systems don't compete directly in cost with cabled networks, when equipment must frequently be moved, microwave can be a cost-effective technology. Capacity can be extremely high, but most data communication systems operate at data rates between 1 and 10 Mbps. Attenuation characteristics are determined by transmitter power, frequency, and antenna size. Properly designed systems are not affected by attenuation under normal operational conditions, but rain and fog can cause attenuation of higher frequencies. Microwave systems are highly susceptible to atmospheric interference and can also be vulnerable to electronic eavesdropping. For this reason, signals transmitted through microwave are frequently encrypted.

Satellite Microwave

Satellite microwave systems relay transmissions through communication satellites that operate in geosynchronous orbits 22,300 miles above the Earth. Satellites orbiting at this distance remain located above a fixed point on the Earth. Earth stations use parabolic antennas (satellite dishes) to communicate with satellites. These satellites can then retransmit signals in broad or narrow beams, depending on the locations set to receive the signals. When the destination is on the opposite side of the Earth, for example, the first satellite can't transmit directly to the receiver and thus must relay the signal through another satellite. Because no cables are required, satellite microwave communication is possible with most remote sites and with mobile devices, which enables transmission with ships at sea and motor vehicles. The distances involved in satellite communication result in an interesting phenomenon: Because all signals must travel 22,300 miles to the satellite and 22,300 miles when returning to a receiver, the time required to transmit a signal is independent of distance. It takes as long to transmit a signal to a receiver in the same state as it does to a receiver a third of the way around the world. The time required for a signal to arrive at its destination is called *propagation delay*. The delays encountered with satellite transmissions range from 0.5 to 5 seconds.

. Unfortunately, satellite communication is extremely expensive. Building and launching a satellite can easily cost in excess of a billion dollars. In most cases, organizations share these costs or purchase services from a commercial provider. AT&T, Hughes Network Services, and Scientific-Atlanta are among firms that sell satellite-based communication services.

Satellite links operate in the low-gigahertz range, typically at 11 to 14 GHz. Costs are extremely high and usually are distributed across many users by selling communication services. Bandwidth is related to cost, and firms can purchase almost any required bandwidth. Typical data rates are 1 to 10 Mbps. Attenuation characteristics depend on frequency, power, and atmospheric conditions. Properly designed systems also take attenuation into account (rain and atmospheric conditions might attenuate higher frequencies). Microwave signals are also sensitive to EMI and electronic eavesdropping, so signals transmitted through microwave frequently are encrypted. Earth stations can be installed by numerous commercial providers. Transmitters operate on licensed frequencies and require an FCC license.

SELECTING TOPOLOGIES

A *topology* is a map of the network. It is a plan for how the cabling will interconnect the nodes and how the nodes will function in relation to one another. Several factors shape the various network topologies. One of the most important is the choice of an access method. An *access method* is a set of rules for sharing the transmission medium.

Access Methods

An access method is a set of rules governing how the network nodes share the transmission medium. The rules for sharing among computers are similar to the rules for sharing among humans in that they both boil down to a pair of fundamental philosophies: First come, first serve, and take turns. These philosophies are the principles that define the two most important types of media access methods:

- **Contention**. In its purest form, contention means that the computers are contending for use of the transmission medium. Any computer in the network can transmit at any time (first come, first serve).

- **Token passing**. The computers take turns using the transmission medium.

As you can imagine, contention-based access methods can give rise to situations in which two or more network nodes try to broadcast at the same time, and the signals collide. Specifications for contention-based access methods include procedures for how to avoid collisions and what to do if a collision occurs. This section introduces the CSMA/CD and CSMA/CA access methods.

On most contention-based networks, the nodes are basically equal. No node has a higher priority than any other node. A new access method called *demand priority,* however, resolves contention and collisions and in so doing accounts for data type priorities.

This section also describes demand priority access.

Contention

In pure contention-based access control, any computer can transmit at any time. This system breaks down when two computers attempt to transmit at the same time, in which case a collision occurs (see Figure 2.21). Eventually, when a network gets busy enough, most attempts to transmit result in collisions, and little effective communication can take place.

Therefore, mechanisms usually are put into place to minimize the effects of collisions. One mechanism is carrier-sensing, whereby each computer listens to the network before attempting to transmit. If the network is busy, the computer refrains from transmitting until the network quiets down. This simple "listen before talking" strategy can significantly reduce collisions. Another mechanism is carrier detection. With this strategy, computers continue to listen to the network as they transmit. If a computer detects another signal that interferes with the signal it's sending, it stops transmitting. Both computers then wait a random amount of time and attempt to retransmit. Unless the network is extremely busy, carrier detection along with carrier sensing can manage a large volume of transmissions.

Carrier detection and carrier sensing used together form the protocol used in all types of Ethernet: Carrier Sense Multiple Access with Collision Detection (CSMA/CD). CSMA/CD limits the size of the network to 2,500 meters. At longer distances, the broadcast-sensing mechanisms don't work—a node at one end can't sense when a node at the other end starts to broadcast.

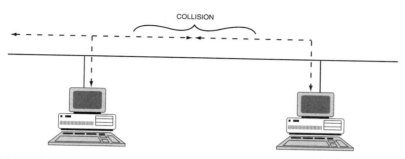

COLLISION

FIGURE 2.21
A collision on a contention-based network.

Apple's LocalTalk network uses the protocol Carrier Sense Multiple Access with Collision Avoidance (CSMA/CA). Collision avoidance uses additional techniques to further reduce the likelihood of collisions. In CSMA/CA, each computer sends a warning that it is about to transmit data, and then the other computers wait for the broadcast. CSMA/CA adds an extra layer of order, thereby reducing collisions, but the warning broadcasts increase network traffic, and the task of constantly listening for warnings increases system load.

Although it sounds as if contention methods are unworkable due to the damage caused by collisions, contention (in particular, CSMA/CD in the form of Ethernet) is the most popular media access control method on LANs. (In fact, no currently employed LAN standards utilize pure contention access control without adding some mechanism to reduce the incidence of collisions.)

Contention is a simple protocol that can operate with simple network software and hardware. Unless traffic levels exceed about 30 percent of bandwidth, contention works quite well. Contention-based networks offer good performance at low cost. Because collisions occur at unpredictable intervals, no computer is guaranteed the capability to transmit at any given time. Contention-based networks are called *probabilistic* because a computer's chance of being permitted to transmit can't be predicted. Collisions increase in frequency as more computers use the network. When too many computers use the network, collisions dominate network traffic, and few frames are transmitted without error.

All computers on a contention-based network are equal. Consequently, it's impossible to assign certain computers higher priorities and, therefore, greater access to the network.

Token Passing

Token passing utilizes a frame called a *token*, which circulates around the network. A computer that needs to transmit must wait until it receives the token, at which time the computer is permitted to transmit. When the computer is finished transmitting, it passes the token frame to the next station on the network. Figure 2.22 shows how token passing is implemented on a Token-Ring network. Token-Ring networks are discussed in greater detail in the later section "Token Ring."

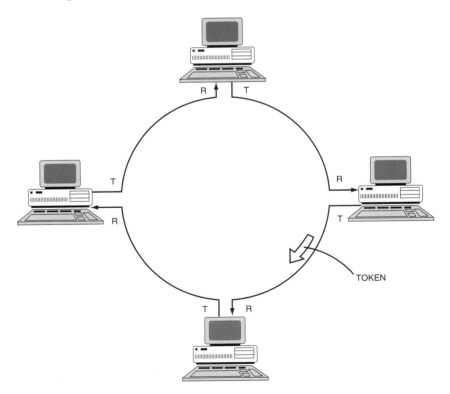

FIGURE 2.22
Token passing.

Several network standards employ token passing access control:

- **Token Ring**. The most common token-passing standard, embodied in IEEE standard 802.5

- **IEEE standard 802.4**. Implemented infrequently. Defines a bus network that also employs token passing.

- **FDDI**. A 100 Mbps fiber-optic network standard that uses token passing and rings in much the same manner as 802.5 Token Ring.

Token-passing methods can use station priorities and other methods to prevent any one station from monopolizing the network. Because each computer has a chance to transmit each time the token travels around the network, each station is guaranteed a chance to transmit at some minimum time interval.

> To use the earlier analogy of people going to work, think of a form of public transportation such as a subway. The client has to wait until the train arrives before boarding. The train doesn't have to contend with traffic (contention) and so on.

Comparing Contention and Token Passing

As an access control mechanism, token passing appears to be clearly superior to contention. You find, however, that Ethernet, by far the dominant LAN standard, has achieved its prominence while firmly wedded to contention access control. Token passing requires a variety of complex control mechanisms in order for it to work well. The necessary hardware is considerably more expensive than the hardware required to implement the much simpler contention mechanisms. The higher cost of token passing networks is difficult to justify unless the special features are required.

Because token-passing networks are designed for high reliability, building network diagnostic and troubleshooting capabilities into the network hardware is common. These capabilities increase the cost of token-passing networks. Organizations must decide whether this additional reliability is worth the extra cost. Conversely, although token-passing networks perform better than contention-based networks when traffic levels are high, contention networks exhibit superior performance under lighter loading conditions. Passing the token around (and other maintenance operations) eats into the available bandwidth. As a result, a 10 Mbps Ethernet and a 16 Mbps Token Ring perform comparably well under light loading conditions, but the Ethernet costs considerably less.

Figure 2.23 illustrates the performance characteristics you can expect from each access control method. (This figure implies that token-passing throughput eventually reaches a zero level, which can't happen, regardless of the loading conditions. Although a station's access to the network might be limited, access is guaranteed with each circuit of the token.)

Demand Priority

Demand priority is an access method used with the new 100 Mbps 100VG-AnyLAN standard. Although demand priority is officially considered a contention-based access method, it is considerably different from the basic CSMA/CD Ethernet. In demand priority, network nodes are connected to hubs, and those hubs are connected to other hubs. Therefore, contention occurs at the hub. (100VG-AnyLAN cables can actually send and receive data at the same time.) Demand priority provides a mechanism for prioritizing data types. If contention occurs, data with a higher priority takes precedence.

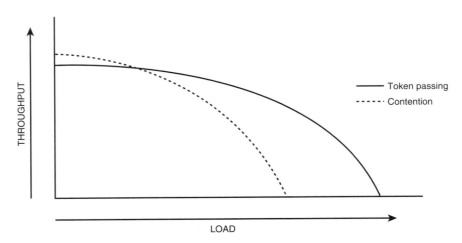

FIGURE 2.23
A comparison of contention and token passing.

Physical and Logical Topologies

A *topology* defines the arrangement of nodes, cables, and connectivity devices that make up the network. Two basic categories form the basis for all discussions of topologies:

- **Physical topology.** Describes the actual layout of the network transmission media.

- **Logical topology.** Describes the logical pathway a signal follows as it passes among the network nodes.

Another way to think about this distinction is that a physical topology defines the way the network looks, and a logical topology defines the way the data passes among the nodes. At first glance this distinction may seem nitpicky, but the physical and logical topologies for a network can be very different. A network with a star physical topology, for example, may actually have a bus or ring logical topology.

In common usage, the word "topology" applies to a complete network definition, which includes the physical and logical topologies and also specifications for elements such as the transmission medium. The term *topology* as used in Microsoft's test objectives for the Networking Essentials exam applies not to the physical and logical topology archetypes described in this section but to the complete network specifications (such as 10Base-T or 10Base5) described in the "Ethernet" and "Token Ring" sections that follow.

Physical and logical topologies can take several forms. The most common and the most important for understanding the Ethernet and Token Ring topologies are

- Bus topologies

- Ring topologies

- Star topologies

The following sections discuss each of these important topology types.

Bus Topologies

A bus physical topology is one in which all devices connect to a common, shared cable (sometimes called the *backbone*). A bus physical topology is shown in Figure 2.24.

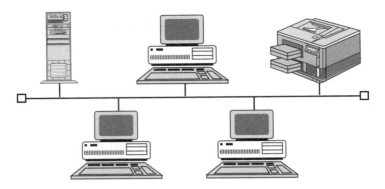

FIGURE 2.24
A bus physical topology.

If you think that the bus topology seems ideally suited for networks that use contention-based access methods such as CSMA/CD, you are correct. Ethernet, the most common contention-based network architecture, typically uses bus as a physical topology.

10Base-T Ethernet networks (described later) use bus as a logical topology but are configured in a star physical topology. Most bus networks broadcast signals in both directions on the backbone cable, allowing all devices to receive the signal directly. Some buses, however, are unidirectional: Signals travel in only one direction and can reach only downstream devices.

A terminator must be placed at the end of the backbone cable to prevent signals from reflecting back on the cable and causing interference. In the case of a unidirectional bus, the cable must be terminated in such a way that signals can reflect back on the cable and reach other devices without causing disruption.

Ring Topologies

Ring topologies are wired in a circle. Each node is connected to its neighbors on either side, and data passes around the ring in one direction only (see Figure 2.25). Each device incorporates a receiver and a transmitter and serves as a repeater that passes the signal to the next device in the ring. Because the signal is regenerated at each device, signal degeneration is low.

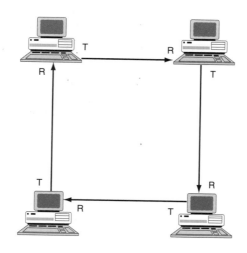

T = TRANSMIT
R = RECEIVE

FIGURE 2.25
A ring topology.

Ring topologies are ideally suited for token-passing access methods. The token gets passed around the ring, and only the node that holds the token can transmit data. Ring physical topologies are quite rare. The ring topology is almost always implemented as a logical topology. Token Ring, for example—the most widespread token-passing network—always arranges the nodes in a physical star (with all nodes connecting to a central hub) but passes data in a logical ring (see Figure 2.26).

Star Topologies

Star topologies require that all devices connect to a central hub (see Figure 2.27). The hub receives signals from other network devices and routes them to the proper destinations. Star hubs can be interconnected to form tree or hierarchical network topologies.

As mentioned earlier, a star physical topology is often used to implement a bus or ring logical topology (see Figure 2.26). In the real world, it is not uncommon to see hybrids, which are mixtures of several different types.

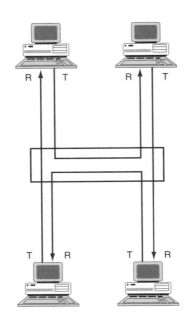

T = TRANSMIT
R = RECEIVE

FIGURE 2.26
A logical ring configured in a physical star.

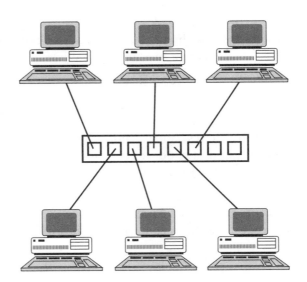

FIGURE 2.27
A star topology.

Ethernet

Ethernet is a very popular local area network architecture based on the CSMA/CD access method. The original Ethernet specification was the basis for the IEEE 802.3 specifications. In present sage, the term *Ethernet* refers to original Ethernet (or Ethernet II, the latest version) as well as the IEEE 802.3 standards. The different varieties of Ethernet networks are commonly referred to as Ethernet topologies. Typically, Ethernet networks use a bus physical topology, although (as mentioned earlier) some varieties of Ethernet, such as 10Base-T, use a star physical topology and a bus logical topology. (Microsoft uses the term *star bus topology* to describe 10Base-T.)

Ethernet networks, depending on the specification, operate at 10 or 100 Mbps using baseband transmission. Each of the IEEE 802.3 specifications prescribes its own cable types.

The next sections in this chapter examine the following Ethernet topologies:

+ 10Base2

+ 10Base5

+ 10Base-T

+ 10Base-FL

+ 100VG-AnyLAN

+ 100Base-X

Note that the name of each Ethernet topology begins with a number (10 or 100). That number specifies the transmission speed for the network. For instance, 10Base5 is designed to operate at 10 Mbps, and 100Base-X operates at 100 Mbps.

Ethernet Frames

Ethernet networks transmit data in small units called *frames*. The size of an Ethernet frame can be anywhere from 64 to 1,518 bytes. Eighteen bytes of the total size is taken up by frame overhead, such as the source and destination addresses, protocol information, and error-checking information.

A typical Ethernet II frame has the following sections:

- **Preamble**. A field that signifies the beginning of the frame.
- **Addresses**. Source and destination addresses for the frame.
- **Type**. A field that designates the Network layer protocol.
- **Data**. The data being transmitted.
- **CRC**. Cyclical Redundancy Check for error checking.

As I mentioned, the term *Ethernet* commonly refers to original Ethernet (which has been updated to Ethernet II) as well as the IEEE 802.3 standards. Ethernet and the 802.3 standards differ in ways significant enough to make standards incompatible in terms of packet formats, however. At the Physical layer, Ethernet and 802.3 are generally compatible in terms of cables, connectors, and electronic devices.

Ethernet generally is used on light-to-medium-traffic networks and performs best when a network's data traffic transmits in short bursts. Ethernet is the most commonly used network standard. It has become especially popular in many university and government installations.

One advantage of the linear bus topology used by most Ethernet networks (this doesn't apply to star bus networks such as 10Base-T) is that the required cabling is minimized because each node doesn't require a separate cable run to the hub. One disadvantage is that a break in the cable or a streaming network adapter card can bring down the entire network. Streaming is more frequently referred to as a *broadcast storm*. A broadcast storm occurs when a network card fails and the transmitter floods the cable with traffic, like a faucet stuck open. At this point, the network becomes unusable.

Ethernet Cabling

You can use a variety of cables to implement Ethernet networks. Ethernet networks traditionally have used coaxial cables of several different types. Fiber-optic cables now are frequently employed to extend the geographic range of Ethernet networks.

The contemporary interest in using twisted-pair wiring has resulted in a scheme for cabling that uses unshielded twisted-pair (UTP): the 10Base-T cabling standard, which uses UTP in a star physical topology. Ethernet remains closely associated with coaxial cable. Two types of coaxial cable still used in small and large environments are Thinnet (10Base2) and Thicknet (10Base5). Thinnet and Thicknet Ethernet networks have different limitations that are based on the Thinnet and Thicknet cable specifications. The best way to remember the requirements is to use the 5-4-3 rule for each cable type. This rule states that the following can appear between any two nodes in the Ethernet network:

- ♦ Up to five segments in a series

- ♦ Up to four concentrators or repeaters

- ♦ Three segments of (coaxial only) cable that contain nodes

See Figure 2.28.

10Base2

The 10Base2 cabling topology (Thinnet) generally uses the onboard transceiver of the network interface card to translate the signals to and from the rest of the network. Thinnet cabling uses BNC T-connectors that directly attach to the network adapter. Each end of the cable should have a terminator, and you must use a grounded terminator on one end.

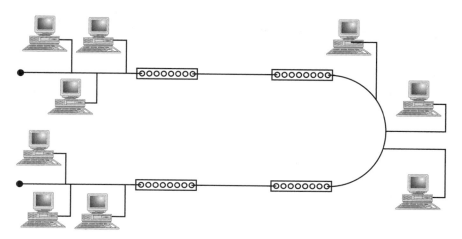

FIGURE 2.28
The 5-4-3 rule.

The main advantage of using 10Base2 in your network is cost. When any given cable segment on the network doesn't have to be run farther than 185 meters (607 feet), 10Base2 is often the cheapest network cabling option. 10Base2 is also relatively simple to connect. Each network node connects directly to the network cable by using a T-connector attached to the network adapter. For a successful installation, you must adhere to several rules in 10Base2 Ethernet environments:

- The minimum cable distance between clients must be 0.5 meters (1.5 feet).

- The T-connector must be connected directly to the network adapter.

- You may not exceed the maximum network segment limitation of 185 meters (607 feet).

- The entire network cabling scheme can't exceed 925 meters (3,035 feet).

- The maximum number of nodes per network segment is 30 (this includes clients and repeaters).

- A 50 ohm terminator must be used on each end of the bus with only one of the terminators having either a grounding strap or a grounding wire that attaches it to the screw holding an electrical outlet cover in place.

- You may not have more than five segments on a network.

- These segments may be connected with a maximum of four repeaters, and only three of the five segments may have network nodes.

Figure 2.29 shows two network segments using 10Base2 cabling.

10Base5

The 10Base5 cabling topology (Thicknet) uses an external transceiver to attach to the network adapter card (see Figure 2.30). The external transceiver clamps to the Thicknet cable. An Attachment Universal Interface (AUI) cable runs from the transceiver to a DIX connector on the back of the network adapter card. As with Thinnet, each network segment must be terminated at both ends, with one end using a grounded terminator.

The components of a Thicknet network are shown in Figure 2.31.

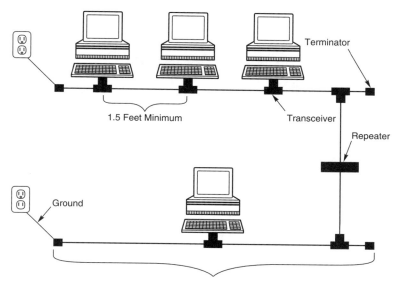

FIGURE 2.29
Two segments using 10Base2 cabling.

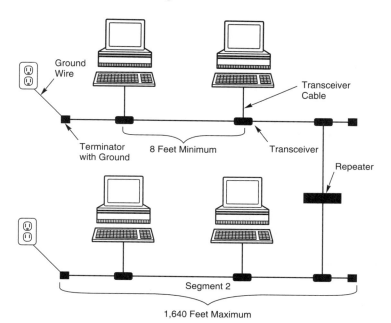

FIGURE 2.30
Two segments using 10Base5 cabling.

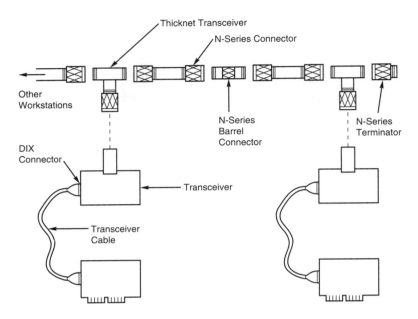

FIGURE 2.31
The components of a Thicknet network.

The primary advantage of 10Base5 is its capability to exceed the cable restrictions that apply to 10Base2. 10Base5 does pose restrictions of its own, however, which you should consider when installing or troubleshooting a 10Base5 network. As with 10Base2 networks, the first consideration when troubleshooting a 10Base5 network should be the established cabling rules and guidelines. You must follow several additional guidelines, along with the 5-4-3 rule, when configuring Thicknet networks:

- ◆ The minimum cable distance between transceivers is 2.5 meters (8 feet).

- ◆ You may not go beyond the maximum network segment length of 500 meters (1,640 feet).

- ◆ The entire network cabling scheme can't exceed 2,500 meters (8,200 feet).

- ◆ One end of the terminated network segment must be grounded.

- ◆ Drop cables (transceiver cables) can be as short as required but can't be longer than 50 meters from transceiver to computer.

- The maximum number of nodes per network segment is 100. (This includes all repeaters.)

- The length of the drop cables (from the transceiver to the computer) is not included in measurements of the network segment length and total network length.

Figure 2.32 shows two segments using Thicknet and the appropriate hardware. In the real world, Thicknet and Thinnet networks are often combined, with a Thicknet backbone merging smaller Thinnet segments.

10Base-T

The trend in wiring Ethernet networks is to use unshielded twisted-pair (UTP) cable. 10Base-T, which uses UTP cable, is one of the most popular implementations for Ethernet. It is based on the IEEE 802.3 standard. 10Base-T supports a data rate of 10 Mbps using baseband.

10Base-T cabling is wired in a star topology. The nodes are wired to a central hub, which serves as a multiport repeater (see Figure 2.33). A 10Base-T network functions logically as a linear bus. The hub repeats the signal to all nodes, and the nodes contend for access to the transmission medium as if they were connected along a linear bus. The cable uses RJ-45 connectors, and the network adapter card can have RJ-45 jacks built into the back of the card.

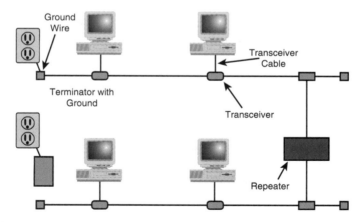

FIGURE 2.32
An example of Thicknet network cabling.

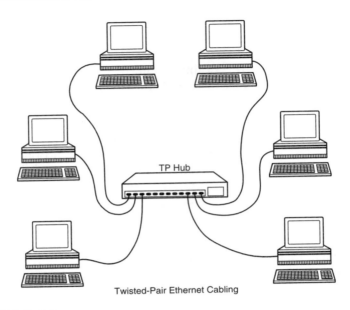

Twisted-Pair Ethernet Cabling

FIGURE 2.33
A 10Base-T network.

10Base-T segments can be connected using coaxial or fiber-optic backbone segments. Some hubs provide connectors for Thinnet and Thicknet cables (in addition to 10Base-T UTP-type connectors).

By attaching a 10Base-T transceiver to the AUI port of the network adapter, you can use a computer set up for Thicknet on a 10Base-T network. The star wiring of 10Base-T provides several advantages, particularly in larger networks. First, the network is more reliable and easier to manage because 10Base-T networks use a concentrator (a centralized wiring hub). These hubs are "intelligent" in that they can detect defective cable segments and route network traffic around them. This capability makes locating and repairing bad cable segments easier.

10Base-T lets you design and build your LAN one segment at a time, growing as your network needs to grow. This capability makes 10Base-T more flexible than other LAN cabling options. 10Base-T is also relatively inexpensive compared to other cabling options. In some cases in which a data-grade phone system is already present in an existing building, the data-grade phone cable can be used for the LAN.

The rules for a 10Base-T network are as follows:

- The maximum number of computers on a LAN is 1,024.

- The cabling should be UTP Category 3, 4, or 5. (Shielded twisted-pair cabling, STP, can be used in place of UTP.)

- The maximum unshielded cable segment length (hub to transceiver) is 100 meters (328 feet).

- The cable distance between computers is 2.5 meters (8 feet).

10Base-FL

10Base-FL is a specification for Ethernet over fiber-optic cables. The 10Base-FL specification calls for a 10 Mbps data rate using baseband.

The most important advantages of fiber-optic cable (and hence, the advantages of 10Base-FL) are long cabling runs (10Base-FL supports a maximum cabling distance of about 2,000 meters) and the elimination of any potential electrical complications.

100VG-AnyLAN

100VG-AnyLAN is defined in the IEEE 802.12 standard. IEEE 802.12 is a standard for transmitting Ethernet and Token Ring packets (IEEE 802.3 and 802.5) at 100 Mbps. 100VG-AnyLAN is sometimes called 100Base-VG. The "VG" stands for "voice grade."

The earlier section "Demand Priority" discussed 100VG-AnyLAN's demand priority access method, which provides for two priority levels when resolving media access conflicts.

100VG-AnyLAN uses a cascaded star topology, which calls for a hierarchy of hubs. Computers are attached to *child hubs,* and the child hubs are connected to higher-level hubs called *parent hubs* (see Figure 2.34).

The maximum length for the two longest cables attached to a 100VG-AnyLAN hub is 250 meters (820 feet). The specified cabling is Category 3, 4, or 5 twisted-pair or fiber-optic. 100VG-AnyLAN is compatible with 10Base-T cabling.

100Base-X

100Base-X uses a star bus topology similar to 10Base-T's. 100Base-X provides a data transmission speed of 100 Mbps using baseband.

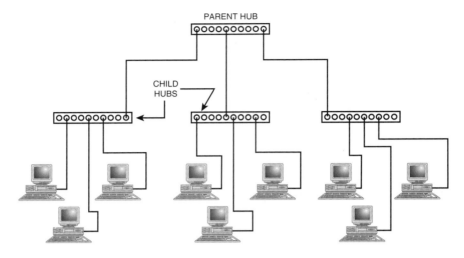

FIGURE 2.34
A cascaded star topology.

The 100Base-X standard provides the following cabling specifications:

- **100Base-TX**. Two twisted pairs of Category 5 UTP or STP.

- **100Base-FX**. Fiber-optic cabling using two-strand cable.

- **100Base-T4**. Four twisted pairs of Category 3, 4, or 5 UTP.

100Base-X is sometimes referred to as "Fast Ethernet." Like 100VG-AnyLAN, 100Base-X provides compatibility with existing 10Base-T systems and thus enables Plug and Play upgrades from 10Base-T.

Token Ring

Token Ring uses a token-passing architecture that adheres to the IEEE 802.5 standard, as described earlier. The topology is physically a star, but Token Ring uses a logical ring to pass the token from station to station. Each node must be attached to a concentrator called a *multistation access unit* (MSAU or MAU).

In the earlier discussion of token passing, it may have occurred to you that if one computer crashes, the others will be left waiting for the token. MSAUs add fault tolerance to the network so that a single failure doesn't stop the whole network. The MSAU can determine when a PC's network adapter fails to transmit and can bypass it.

Token Ring network interface cards can run at 4 Mbps or 16 Mbps. Although 4 Mbps cards can run only at that data rate, 16 Mbps cards can be configured to run at 4 or 16 Mbps. All cards on a given network ring must run at the same rate.

As shown in Figure 2.35, each node acts as a repeater that receives tokens and data frames from its nearest active upstream neighbor (NAUN). After the node processes a frame, the frame transmits downstream to the next attached node. Each token makes at least one trip around the entire ring and then returns to the originating node. Workstations that indicate problems send a beacon to identify an address of the potential failure.

Token-Ring Cabling

Traditional Token Ring networks use twisted-pair cable. The following are standard IBM cable types for Token Ring:

- ◆ **Type 1.** A braided shield surrounds two twisted pairs of solid copper wire. Type 1 is used to connect terminals and distribution panels or to connect between different wiring closets that are located in the same building. Type 1 uses two STPs of solid-core 22 AWG wire for long, high data-grade transmissions within the building's walls. The maximum cabling distance is 101 meters (331 feet).

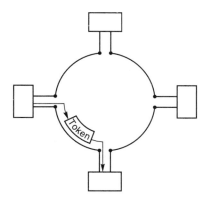

FIGURE 2.35
The operation of a Token Ring.

◆ **Type 2**. Type 2 uses a total of six twisted pairs. Two are STPs (for networking), and four are UTPs (for telephone systems). This cable is used for the same purposes as Type 1, but it lets both voice and data cables be included in a single cable run. The maximum cabling distance is 100 meters (328 feet).

◆ **Type 3**. Used as an alternative to Type 1 and Type 2 cable because of its reduced cost, Type 3 has unshielded twisted-pair copper with a minimum of two twists per inch. Type 3 has four UTPs of 22 or 24 AWG solid-core wire for networks or telephone systems. Type 3 can't be used for 16 Mbps Token Ring networks. It is used primarily for long, low data-grade transmissions within walls. Signals don't travel as fast as with Type 1 cable because Type 3 doesn't have the shielding that Type 1 uses. The maximum cabling distance (according to IBM) is 45 meters (about 148 feet). Some vendors specify cabling distances of up to 150 meters (500 feet).

Type 3 cabling (UTP) is the most popular transmission medium for Token Ring. A Token Ring network using Type 3 (UTP) cabling can support up to 72 computers. A Token Ring network using STP cabling can support up to 260 computers.

The minimum distance between computers or between MSAUs is 2.5 meters (8 feet). A *patch cable* is a cable that connects MSAUs. Patch cables are typically IBM Type 6 cables that come in standard lengths of 8, 30, 75, and 150 feet. (A Type 6 cable consists of two shielded 26-AWG twisted pairs.) You can also get patch cables in custom lengths.

You can use patch cables to extend the length of Type 3 cables or to connect computers to MSAUs. Patch cables have an IBM connector at each end. Token Ring adapter cables have an IBM data connector at one end and a nine-pin connector at the other end. Adapter cables connect client and server network adapters to other network components that use IBM data connectors. The type of connectors you'll need for a Token Ring network depends on the type of cabling you're using. Type 3 cabling uses RJ-11 or RJ-45 connectors.

(Media filters, if necessary, can convert the network adapter to RJ-11 or RJ-45 format.) Meanwhile, Type 1 and 2 cabling use IBM Type A connectors.

Token Ring networks come in a few sizes and designs. A small movable Token Ring system supports up to 12 MSAUs and uses Type 6 cable to attach clients and servers to IBM Model 8228 MSAUs. Type 6 is flexible but has limited distance capabilities. The characteristics of Type 6 cable make it suitable for small networks and patch cords.

A large immovable system supports up to 260 clients and file servers with up to 33 MSAUs. This network configuration uses IBM Type 1 or Type 2 cable. The large nonmovable system also involves other wiring needs, such as punch panels or distribution panels, equipment racks for MSAUs, and wiring closets to contain the components just listed.

The MSAU is the central cabling component for IBM Token Ring networks. The 8228 MSAU, shown in Figure 2.36, was the original wiring hub developed by IBM for Token Ring networks. Figure 2.36 shows 8228 MSAUs.

Each 8228 has 10 connectors, eight of which accept cables to clients or servers. The other connectors are labeled RI (ring in) and RO (ring out). The RI and RO connectors are used to connect multiple 8228s to form larger networks. 8228s are mechanical devices that consist of relays and connectors. Their purpose is to switch clients into and out of the network. Each port is controlled by a relay powered by a voltage sent to the MSAU from the client. When an 8228 is first set up, each of these relays must be initialized with the setup tool that is shipped with the unit. Insert the setup tool into each port and hold it there until a light indicates that the port is properly initialized.

Figure 2.36 shows an example of a network cabling several clients and MSAUs. The distances noted in the figure are based on the rules for the small movable cabling system.

When you connect a Token Ring network, make sure you do the following:

1. Initialize each port in the 8228 MSAU by using the setup tool shipped with the MSAU.

2. If you're using more than one MSAU, connect the RO port of each MSAU with the RI port of the next MSAU in the loop. Complete the loop so that the MSAUs form a circle or ring.

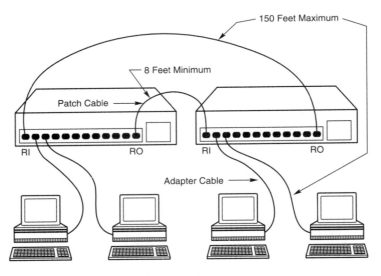

Token Ring Cabling

FIGURE 2.36
An example of Token Ring cabling using MSAUs.

Passing Data on Token Rings

As this chapter has already noted, a frame called a *token* perpetually circulates around a Token Ring. The computer that holds the token has control of the transmission medium. Here is the actual process:

1. A computer in the ring captures the token.

2. If the computer has data to transmit, it holds the token and transmits a data frame. A Token Ring data frame contains the fields listed in Table 2.2.

3. Each computer in the ring checks to see if it is the intended recipient of the frame.

4. When the frame reaches the destination address, the destination PC copies the frame to a receive buffer, updates the frame status field of the data frame (see step 2), and puts the frame back on the ring.

5. When the computer that originally sent the frame receives it from the ring, it acknowledges a successful transmission, takes the frame off the ring, and places the token back on the ring.

TABLE 2.2

TOKEN RING DATA FRAME FIELDS

Field	Description
Start delimiter	Marks the start of the frame.
Access control	Specifies the frame's priority. Also specifies whether the frame is a token or a data frame.
Frame control	Media Access Control information.
Destination address	The address of the receiving computer.
Source address	The address of the sending computer.
Data	The data being transmitted.
Frame check sequence	Error-checking information (CRC).
End delimiter	Marks the end of the frame.
Frame status	Tells whether the destination address was located and whether the frame was recognized.

The Beaconing Process

Generally, the first station that is powered up on a Token Ring network automatically becomes what is called the *active monitor station.* Its responsibility is to identify itself to the next active downstream station as the active monitor station and to tell that station to identify itself to its next active downstream station. The active monitor station sends this beacon announcement every seven seconds.

After each station announces itself to its next active downstream neighbor, the announcing station becomes the nearest active upstream neighbor (NAUN) to the downstream station. Each station on a Token Ring network has an upstream neighbor as well as a downstream neighbor.

After each station becomes aware of its NAUN, the beaconing process continues every seven seconds. If for some reason a station doesn't receive one of its expected seven-second beaconed announcements from its upstream neighbor, it attempts to notify the network of the lack of contact from the upstream neighbor. It sends a message to the network ring, which includes the following:

- The sending station's network address

- The receiving NAUN's network address

- The beacon type

From this information, the ring can determine which station might be having a problem and then attempt to fix the problem without disrupting the entire network. This process is known as *autoreconfiguration*. If this process proves unsuccessful, manual correction becomes necessary. Figure 2.37 shows a Token Ring network utilizing the beaconing process.

PROTOCOL CHOICES

At A Glance: Networking Protocols

Protocol	Installed on NT	Main Benefits	Main Drawback
Data Link Control (DLC)	By the administrator after installation	Provides connectivity to IBM mainframes and AS400s	Not used by any Microsoft clients
AppleTalk	By the administrator after installation	Allows Macintosh clients to communicate with NT Server	Not used by any Microsoft clients
IPX (NWLink)	By the administrator	Needed for compatibility with NetWare	Used only for NetWare compatibility
TCP/IP	By default	Routable, language of the Internet, industry standard	Management
NFS (Network File System)	N/A	Networking language inherent in Unix operating systems	Support for Windows NT's SMB not included
SMB (Server Message Blocks)	Inherent	Windows operating systems networking language	Support for NFS not included

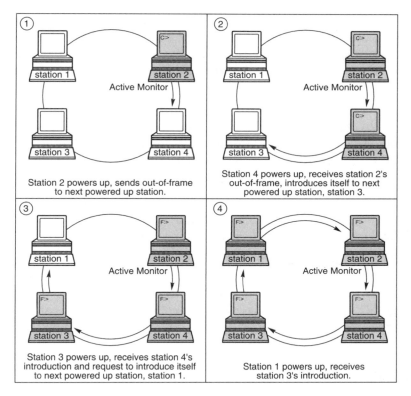

FIGURE 2.37
Token-Ring beaconing.

Protocols are standards or languages that computers use to talk to each other in a network. Microsoft Windows NT Server 4 installs TCP/IP as the default protocol and uses SMB (Server Message Blocks) as the networking language.

TCP/IP is the protocol that was originally used with the Unix hosts. Unix hosts were almost exclusively the hosts comprising the Internet until a few years ago. With the growth in popularity of the Internet, and the need to communicate using a common protocol, TCP/IP has quickly become the de facto standard used for networking today. It benefits greatly from being easily routed and available for all platforms. Its only real requirement is that each host must have a unique IP address. TCP/IP supports DHCP, DNS, and WINS, all of which are discussed in the next section.

NWLink is a protocol compatible with IPX/SPX—the networking protocol used by NetWare servers. It is needed on the Windows NT Server if you must service NetWare clients or interact with NetWare servers or if you're attempting to migrate from NetWare to NT. NWLink is also easily routed (as is IPX/SPX).

Data Link Control (DLC) is primarily used as the SNA component of Microsoft BackOffice to communicate with IBM mainframes and AS400s. It also has one additional use: Many HP network printers also use DLC, although they can be (and often are) converted to TCP/IP with the inclusion of a JetDirect card.

AppleTalk is the protocol that Macintosh computers use. Installing this protocol on the NT Server allows Mac users to access files and printers on the server. It also lets NT clients print to AppleTalk printers.

NetBEUI is the protocol originally used in Microsoft's Windows for Workgroups and LAN Manager networking products. Ideal for department-sized LANs, it can't be routed (although it can be used with a bridge). It's primarily used now only for compatibility with existing networks.

CONNECTIVITY DEVICES

Connectivity devices to be aware of for the Networking Essentials exam include repeaters, bridges, routers, brouters, and gateways. All of these hardware items were discussed in detail in Chapter 1, "Standards and Terminology."

WAN CONNECTION SERVICES

At A Glance: WAN Technologies

Technology	Name	Feature
ATM	Asynchronous Transfer Mode	155 Mbps to 622 MBps packet switching with all data being exactly 53-byte cells.
Frame Relay	N/A	A point-to-point system across leased lines through the use of a bridge or router.
ISDN	Integrated Services Digital Network	A three-channel dial up 128 Kbps technology that performs link management and signaling.
X.25	N/A	Connects at low cost remote terminals to mainframe hosts through Public Data Networks (PDNs) and does error-checking (which slows it down).

There are four Wide Area Network technologies to be aware of for the Networking Essentials exam. The following sections explore them in detail.

ATM

Asynchronous Transfer Mode (ATM) is a high-bandwidth switching technology developed by the ITU Telecommunications Standards Sector (ITU-TSS). An organization called the ATM Forum is responsible for defining ATM implementation characteristics. ATM can be layered on other Physical layer technologies, such as Fiber Distributed Data Interface (FDDI) and SONET. The relationships of these protocols to the OSI model are shown in Figure 2.38.

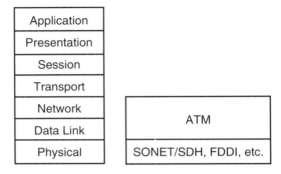

FIGURE 2.38
The relationship of ATM to the OSI model.

Several characteristics distinguish ATM from other switching technologies. ATM is based on fixed-length 53-byte cells, whereas other technologies employ frames that vary in length to accommodate different amounts of data. Because ATM cells are uniform in length, switching mechanisms can operate with a high level of efficiency. This high efficiency results in high data transfer rates. Some ATM systems can operate at an incredible rate of 622 Mbps; a typical working speed for an ATM is around 155 Mbps.

The unit of transmission for ATM is called a *cell*. All cells are 53 bytes long and consist of a 5-byte header and 48 bytes of data. The 48-byte data size was selected by the standards committee as a compromise to suit both audio- and data-transmission needs. Audio information, for instance, must be delivered with little latency (delay) to maintain a smooth flow of sound. Audio engineers therefore preferred a small cell so that cells would be more readily available when needed. For data, however, large cells reduce the overhead required to deliver a byte of information.

Asynchronous delivery is another distinguishing feature of ATM. *Asynchronous* refers to the characteristic of ATM in which transmission time slots don't occur periodically but are granted at irregular intervals. ATM uses a technique called *label multiplexing*, which allocates time slots on demand. Traffic that is time-critical, such as voice or video, can be given priority over data traffic that can be delayed slightly with no ill effect. Channels are identified by cell labels, not by specific time slots. A high-priority transmission need not be held until its next time slot allocation. Instead, it might be required to wait only until the current 53-byte cell has been transmitted.

Devices communicate on ATM networks by establishing a virtual path, which is identified by a virtual path identifier (VPI). Within this virtual path, virtual circuits can be established, which are in turn associated with virtual circuit identifiers (VCIs). The VPI and VCI together make up a 3-byte field included in the cell header.

ATM is a relatively new technology, so only a few suppliers provide the equipment necessary to support it. (ATM networks must use ATM-compatible switches, routers, and other connectivity devices.) Other networks, such as a routed Ethernet, require a 6-byte physical address as well as a network address to uniquely identify each device on an internetwork. An ATM can switch cells with 3-byte identifiers because VPIs and VCIs apply only to a given device-to-device link. Each ATM switch can assign different VPIs and VCIs for each link, and up to 16 million circuits can be configured for any given device-to-device link.

Although ATM was developed primarily as a WAN technology, it has many characteristics of value for high-performance LANs. An interesting advantage of ATM is that ATM makes it possible to use the same technology for both LANs and WANs. Some disadvantages, however, include the cost, the limited availability of the equipment, and the present lack of people who have expertise in ATM due to its recent arrival.

NOTE

Two other evolving technologies related to ATM show promise:

Synchronous Optical Network (SONET). Bell Communications Research developed SONET, which has been accepted as an ANSI standard. As the "optical" in the name implies, SONET is a standard for communication over fiber-optic networks. Data rates for SONET are organized in a hierarchy based on the Optical Carrier (OC) speed and the corresponding Synchronous Transport Signals (STS) employed. The basic OC and STS data rate is 51.84 Mbps, but higher data rates are provided in multiples of the basic rate. Thus, OC-48 is 48X51.84 Mbps, or 2488.32 Mbps.

Switched Multimegabit Digital Service (SMDS). Developed by Bell Communications Research in 1991, SMDS technology is related to ATM in that it transports data in 53-byte cells. SMDS is a connectionless Data Link layer service that supports cell switching at data rates of 1.544 to 45 Mbps. IEEE 802.6 (DQDB metropolitan area network) is the primary Physical layer standard employed with SMDS, although other Physical layer standards are supported.

Frame Relay

Frame Relay was designed to support the Broadband Integrated Services Digital Network (B-ISDN). The specifications for Frame Relay address some of the limitations of X.25. As with X.25, Frame Relay is a packet-switching network service, but Frame Relay was designed around newer, faster fiber-optic networks.

Unlike X.25, Frame Relay assumes a more reliable network. This lets Frame Relay eliminate much of the X.25 overhead required to provide reliable service on less-reliable networks. Frame Relay relies on higher-level protocol layers to provide flow and error control.

Frame Relay typically is implemented as a public data network and therefore is regarded as a WAN protocol. The relationship of Frame Relay to the OSI model is shown in Figure 2.39. Notice that the scope of Frame Relay is limited to the Physical and Data Link layers.

Frame Relay provides permanent virtual circuits, which supply permanent virtual pathways for WAN connections. Frame Relay services typically are implemented at line speeds from 56 Kbps up to 1.544 Mbps (T1).

Customers typically purchase access to a specific amount of bandwidth on a Frame-Relay service. This bandwidth is called the *committed information rate* (CIR), a data rate for which the customer is guaranteed access. Customers might be permitted to access higher data rates on a temporary pay-per-use basis. This arrangement allows customers to tailor their network access costs based on their bandwidth requirements.

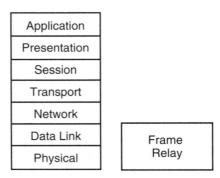

FIGURE 2.39
The relationship of Frame Relay to the OSI model.

To use Frame Relay, you must have special Frame Relay-compatible connectivity devices (such as Frame Relay-compatible routers and bridges).

ISDN and B-ISDN

Integrated Services Digital Network (ISDN) is a group of ITU (CCITT) standards designed to provide voice, video, and data-transmission services on digital telephone networks. ISDN uses multiplexing to support multiple channels on high-bandwidth circuits. The relationship of the ISDN protocols to the OSI reference model is shown in Figure 2.40.

The original idea behind ISDN was to let existing phone lines carry digital communications. Thus, ISDN is more like traditional telephone service than some of the other WAN services. It's intended as a dial-up service and not as a permanent 24-hour connection.

ISDN separates the bandwidth into channels (see the following note for more information). Basic ISDN uses three channels. Two channels (called B channels) carry the digital data at 64 Kbps. A third channel (called the D channel) provides link and signaling information at 16 Kbps. Basic Rate ISDN thus is referred to as 2B+D. A single PC transmitting through ISDN can use both B channels simultaneously, providing a maximum data rate of 128 Kbps (or higher with compression). The larger-scale Primary Rate ISDN supports 23 64 Kbps B channels and one 64 Kbps D channel.

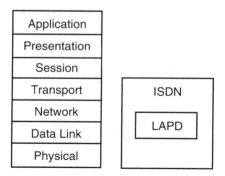

FIGURE 2.40
The relationship of ISDN to the OSI model.

N O T E A variety   of ISDN channel types are defined. These channel types, often called *bit pipes,* provide different types and levels of service. The following list details the various channels:

♦ **A channel.** Provides 4 KHz analog telephone service.

♦ **B channels.** Support 64 Kbps digital data.

♦ **C channels.** Support 8 or 16 Kbps digital data, generally for out-of-band signaling.

♦ **D channels.** Support 16 or 64 Kbps digital data, also for out-of-band signaling. D channels support the following subchannels:

• p subchannels support low-bandwidth packet data.

• s subchannels are used for signaling (such as call setup).

• t subchannels support telemetry data (such as utility meters).

♦ **E channels.** Provide 64 Kbps service used for internal ISDN signaling.

♦ **H channels.** Provide 384, 1,536, or 1,920 Kbps digital service.

ISDN functions   as a data-transmission service only. Acknowledged, connectionless, full-duplex service is provided at the Data Link layer by the LAPD protocol, which operates on the D channel.

Broadband ISDN (B-ISDN) is a refinement of ISDN that is defined to support higher-bandwidth applications, such as video, imaging, and multimedia. Physical layer support for B-ISDN is provided by Asynchronous Transfer Mode (ATM) and the Synchronous Optical Network (SONET). Typical B-ISDN data rates are 51 Mbps, 155 Mbps, and 622 Mbps over fiber-optic media.

X.25

X.25 is a packet-switching network standard developed by the International Telegraph and Telephone Consultative Committee (CCITT), which has been renamed the International Telecommunications Union (ITU). This standard, referred to as

Recommendation X.25, was introduced in 1974 and is now implemented most commonly in WANs.

As shown in Figure 2.41, X.25 is one level of a three-level stack that spans the Network, Data Link, and Physical layers. The middle layer, Link Access Procedures-Balanced (LAPB), is a bit-oriented, full-duplex, synchronous Data Link layer LLC protocol. Physical layer connectivity is provided by a variety of standards, including X.21, X.21bis, and V.32.

X.25 packet-switching networks provide the options of permanent or switched virtual circuits. Although a datagram protocol (which was unreliable) was supported until 1984, X.25 is now required to provide reliable service and end-to-end flow control. Because each device on a network can operate more than one virtual circuit, X.25 must provide error and flow control for each virtual circuit.

At the time X.25 was developed, this flow control and error checking were essential, because X.25 was developed around relatively unreliable telephone line communications. The drawback is that error checking and flow control slow down X.25. Generally, X.25 networks are implemented with line speeds up to 64 Kbps. These speeds are suitable for the file transfer and terminal activity that comprised the bulk of network traffic when X.25 was defined. However, such speeds are inadequate to provide LAN-speed services, which typically require speeds of 1 Mbps or better. Therefore, X.25 networks are poor choices for providing LAN application services in a WAN environment. One advantage of X.25, however, is that it is an established standard that is used internationally.

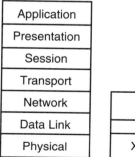

FIGURE 2.41
The relationship of X.25 to the OSI model.

Figure 2.42 shows a typical X.25 configuration. In X.25 parlance, a computer or terminal is called *data terminal equipment* (DTE). A DTE could also be a gateway providing access to a local network. *Data communications equipment* (DCE) provides access to the *packet-switched network* (PSN). A PSE is a *packet-switching exchange*, also called a *switch* or *switching node*.

The X.25 protocol oversees the communication between the DTE and the DCE. A device called a *packet assembler/disassembler* (PAD) translates asynchronous input from the DTE into packets suitable for the PDN.

Public Telephone Lines

Although it isn't an objective for the exam, every real-world administrator needs a basic understanding of leased public phone lines. The possibilities available include the following:

- T1
- T3
- Fractional and multiple T1 or T3
- Digital Data Service
- Switched 56

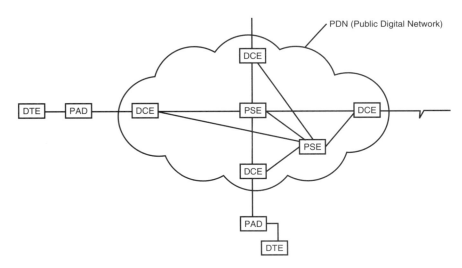

FIGURE 2.42
An X.25 network.

A very popular digital line, T1, provides point-to-point connections and transmits a total of 24 channels across two wire pairs—one pair for sending and one for receiving—for a transmission rate of 1.544 Mbps. T3 is similar to T1, but it has an even higher capacity. In fact, a T3 line can transmit at up to 45 Mbps.

Very few private networks require the capacity of a T3 line, and many don't even need the full capacity of a T1. The channels of a T1 or T3 line thus can be subdivided or combined for fractional or multiple levels of service. For instance, one channel of a T1's 24-channel bandwidth can transmit at 64 Kbps. This single-channel service is called DS-0. DS-1 service is a full T1 line. DS-1C is two T1 lines, DS-2 is four T1 lines, and DS-3 is a full T3 line (equivalent to 28 T1s). A level of service called T4 is equivalent to 168 T1 lines.

Digital Data Service (DDS) is a very basic form of digital service. DDS transmits point-to-point at 2.4, 4.8, 9.6, or 56 Kbps. In its most basic form, DDS provides a dedicated line. A special service related to DDS, Switched 56, offers a dial-up version of the 56 Kbps DDS. With Switched 56, users can dial other Switched 56 sites and pay for only the connect time.

WHAT IS IMPORTANT TO KNOW

The following list summarizes the chapter and accentuates the key concepts to memorize for the exam:

- The category of the cable directly affects the speed.
- Category 3 can go to 10 MBps.
- Category 4 can go to 16 MBps.
- Category 5 can go to 100 MBps.
- With bus topology, a single cable connects all the computers in a single line.
- With star topology, the computers are connected to a hub through cable segments.
- In ring topology, all the computers are on a single wire that forms a loop.
- Wireless media can be of several different types. The four most common, ranked in order of cost, are infrared, laser, narrow-band radio, and spread-spectrum radio.
- ATM (Asynchronous Transfer Mode) uses fixed-length 53-byte packets (which ATM advocates call cells) and sends them across the internetwork.

▶ Choose an administrative plan to meet specified needs, including performance management, account management, and security.

▶ Choose a disaster recovery plan for various situations.

▶ Given the manufacturer's documentation for the network adapter, install, configure, and resolve hardware conflicts for multiple network adapters in a token-ring or Ethernet network.

▶ Implement a NetBIOS naming scheme for all computers on a given network.

▶ Select the appropriate hardware and software tools to monitor trends in the network.

C H A P T E R 3

Implementation

ADMINISTRATIVE PLANS

Administrative planning can be divided into three categories:

- Performance
- Accounts
- Security

Performance is examined in the last part of this chapter. First, we will look at account planning/management and security, using Windows NT 4.0 as the model.

Understanding User Accounts

Windows NT has two ways for users to get rights and permissions to resources:

- They are explicitly assigned a right or permission through their accounts.
- They are members of a group that has a right or permission.

Windows NT user accounts, with their unique identifiers, allow a user to log on to the Windows NT network. The account/password combination is the user's ticket to all the resources on the Windows NT network.

Windows NT user accounts are created in User Manager for Domains. Before you create a new account, the user running User Manager for Domains must be a member of either the Administrators local group or the Account Operators local group.

User Properties

Each user has several property pages. When you're creating a new user, the first screen, shown in Figure 3.1, allows for individual settings.

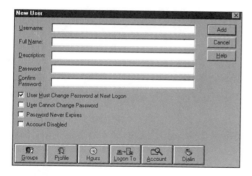

FIGURE 3.1
The New User dialog box.

The New User dialog box displays such items as the user's name and password and how to handle the changing of that password:

♦ **Username.** This is the name that each user will use to log in to the network. This name must be unique in the domain. The name must be no longer than 20 characters and can't contain " / \ [ ] : ; | = , + * ? < > as characters. The goal of enterprise networking is for each user in the enterprise to have only *one* user account.

♦ **Full Name.** This allows for the display of the user's full name. This can be used as a sort setting by selecting View | Sort by Full Name.

♦ **Description.** This setting is copied from account to account if used as a template. It is used to further describe a user.

♦ **Password/Confirm Password.** The password for the user can be up to 14 characters long. If the user is using a Windows logon (versus a Client for Microsoft Networks logon), the password is also case-sensitive. If the user is using a Windows 95 or lower system, the password is not case sensitive.

Of the five properties at the top of the dialog box, only the description will be copied from account to account. All other settings must be re-entered for a copied user.

The other settings in the New User dialog box relate to how passwords will be handled:

♦ **User Must Change Password at Next Logon.** This approach forces the user to change his password when he next logs on to the network.

- **User Cannot Change Password.** This option is used in higher-security networks where users are assigned passwords for their accounts.

- **Password Never Expires.** This setting overrides the account policy of password expiration and should be used only for service accounts in Windows NT.

- **Account Disabled.** This setting prevents the user from using this account.

- **Account Locked Out.** This setting is active only if a user's account has been locked out by the operating system for failing the Account Lockout settings. To reactivate an account, clear the checkbox for this setting.

Group Properties

The Group properties are used to assign the user whose account you are modifying to various groups. To access the dialog box shown in Figure 3.2, click the Groups button in the New User dialog box.

This dialog box allows the assignment of users only to global and local groups in the same domain as the user (generally, users are assigned to global groups). To assign a user to a group in a different domain, you must use the properties of the local group in that domain.

The Primary Group option at the bottom of the dialog box is used by Services for Macintosh. You can designate a primary global group for the account. The primary group is also used when a user running a POSIX application logs on.

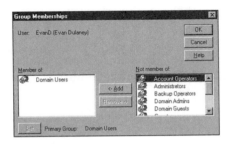

FIGURE 3.2
The Group Memberships dialog box.

User Environment Profile

The User Environment Profile page, shown in Figure 3.3, is one of the main configuration pages used in an enterprise network. To get there, click the Profile button in the New User dialog box.

This dialog box allows the administrator to configure the following as centrally located:

- ◆ User profile path
- ◆ Login script
- ◆ Home directory

The main purpose of centrally locating these options is to have all of these items stored on a central server. Having the users store their profiles and home directories centrally makes the process of backing up their data more manageable.

Logon Hours Properties

The Logon Hours dialog box, shown in Figure 3.4, allows the administrator to set what hours the user account is allowed access to the network. To reach this dialog box, click the Hours button in the New User dialog box.

If the user attempts to log on to the network during nonallowed hours, he will see a dialog box stating that he isn't allowed to log on during these hours.

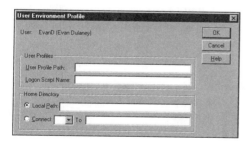

FIGURE 3.3
The User Environment Profile dialog box.

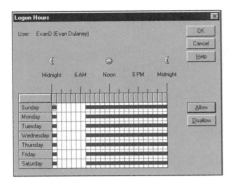

FIGURE 3.4
The Logon Hours dialog box.

If the user is currently logged on and his logon hours restriction kicks into effect, he won't be able to connect to any further net shares. Likewise, he won't be able to use any of his current shares. If the user logs out, he won't be allowed to log on to the network until the next block of time when he is allowed to log in. Realize that this is the default setting. You can change this to forcibly disconnect clients by selecting that option under Policies Account in User Manager for Domains.

Log on to Properties

The Logon Workstations dialog box, shown in Figure 3.5, is used to restrict users to working at specific workstations. To get to this dialog box, click the Logon To button in the New User dialog box.

You can specify up to eight computer names. They are entered as the computer name, not UNC format. For example, you would type PORT-LAND, not \\PORTLAND.

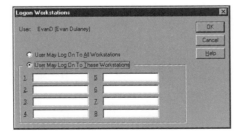

FIGURE 3.5
The Logon Workstations dialog box.

Account Properties

The Account Information dialog box, shown in Figure 3.6, is used by an administrator to define one of two things:

- Setting an account expiration date. Used for any temporary employees for whom the administrator would know when the account should stop being accessible.

- Setting whether the account is global or local. Global is the default.

To get to this dialog box, click the Account button in the New User dialog box.

Dialin Properties

The Dialin Information dialog box, shown in Figure 3.7, allows the administrator to determine which users are granted dial-in access to the network and whether callback security is to be implemented. To get there, click the Dialin button in the New User dialog box.

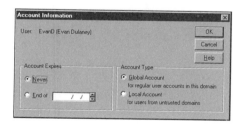

FIGURE 3.6
The Account Information dialog box.

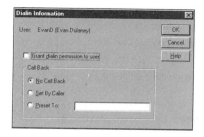

FIGURE 3.7
The Dialin Information dialog box.

If No Call Back is selected, the user will immediately be able to use network resources. This setting is commonly used in low-security networks and for users working out of hotel rooms.

If Set By Caller is selected, the user will be prompted to enter the phone number where he is currently located, and the Remote Access Server will call him back at that number.

If Preset To is configured, the user will dial in to the office network. Upon connecting, the line will be dropped, and the user will be called back at a predefined phone number.

Template Accounts

As an administrator, you should consider creating template user accounts for your various types of users. This would allow you to quickly create new user accounts when required. These template accounts should be disabled to prevent their use on the network for network access.

To use the template account to your advantage, just select the template account in User Manager for Domains and create a copy of it by selecting User | Copy (or press F8). This will copy all properties of the template account except for the following:

- Username
- Full Name
- Password
- Confirm Password
- Account Disabled

Template accounts work best when you make use of the %USERNAME% environment variable for both the User Profile Path and the Home Directory. This will also enable the option User Must Change Password at Next Logon while disabling the Account Disabled box.

One last note: It's always preferable to rename an account than to copy an existing account, because renaming keeps the same permissions and descriptions as the original. Once deleted, group and user accounts can't be undeleted. They must be re-created and permissions and restrictions manually assigned. You can rename accounts very easily, because they are really identified to the system by a Security Identifier (SID).

At the risk of redundancy, to create templates, the system administrator creates an account (just like a standard user account), sets all the groups, hours, dial-in, and so on, and then only has to copy the account and change the fields that differ.

Differences Between Global and Local Groups

One of the most difficult enterprise technologies to get a handle on is the difference between *global* groups and *local* groups. In an enterprise network, the acronym AGLP is used to define the use of global and local groups. AGLP stands for Accounts/Global Groups/Local Groups/Permissions. This means that when you want to assign permissions to any resource, you must follow these steps:

1. Make sure that user accounts exist for each user who will need access to the resource.

2. Assign all user accounts to a common global group. If the users are spread across multiple domains, you will have to create a global group in each domain. This is because global groups can only contain users from the domain in which they are located. Always use a preexisting global group if one exists, and create new global groups only if you have to.

3. Assign the global groups from each domain to a local group in the domain where the resource exists. If the resource is on a Windows NT Domain Controller, it is created on a domain controller. If the resource is on a Windows NT Workstation or Windows NT Member Server, the local group is created on that system's local account database.

4. Assign the necessary permissions to the local group.

Local groups are the only groups that should be assigned permissions. When assigning local group permissions, the administrator should always determine if there is an existing local group with the appropriate permissions. For example, suppose you want to grant a user the ability to create new users or change group memberships. The Account Operators local group already has these permissions, so there is no reason to create a new local group to perform this task.

The Administrators group is found on all Windows NT-class computers. This group can manage any and all aspects of the Windows NT domain. The initial membership in the Administrators group is the precreated Administrator account and the Domain Admins global group.

The Backup Operators local group's members have the right to back up and restore any files on the system. This right supersedes any permissions assigned to these files and directories. Backup Operators can also shut down a server.

The Guests local group has the ability to grant access to specific resources to guests of the domain. The initial membership in the Guests local group is the Domain Guests global group from the domain.

The Replicator group is used by the Directory Replicator service. Membership in this group lets a member be involved in the process of maintaining a directory structure and its contents on multiple domain controllers.

The Users local group contains the global group Domain Users. This group is most often used when increasing the security on a Windows NT domain. Rather than keeping the default share and NTFS permissions, use the local group users instead of everyone.

Managing Security

As shown in Figure 3.8, user rights are used to define security when the activity to be performed by a user can't be associated with one particular object. Several predefined user rights can grant these nondiscretionary levels of access to the system. To implement the User Rights policy, from User Manager for Domains, select Policies | User Rights.

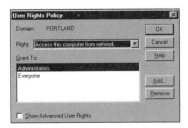

FIGURE 3.8
The User Rights Policy dialog box.

Administering Account Policies

Before you start implementing user accounts, one of the most important policies to set is your account policy, as shown in Figure 3.9.

These policies affect every account in the domain. You can't pick and choose which ones are affected. The account policies define how password changes will be handled and what happens when a user improperly enters his password.

The Password portion of the Account Policy dialog box determines your rules for password security. Password options include the following:

- Maximum Password Age
- Minimum Password Age
- Minimum Password Length
- Password Uniqueness
- Account lockout
- Lockout Duration
- Handling remote users whose logon hours have expired
- Changing passwords

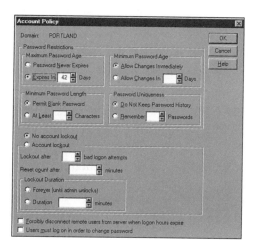

FIGURE 3.9
The Account Policy dialog box and default settings.

When a maximum password age is used, users get a warning 14 days before the password is set to expire. The default expiration value is 42, but it can be any number of days between 1 and 999.

Minimum Password Age can also be any number between 1 and 999. It requires users to keep a password, after having made a change, for the number of days set.

Minimum Password Length forces users to choose a password of up to 14 characters (although 6 to 8 characters is best for most implementations).

Password Uniqueness keeps a history of passwords that the user has used and won't let him use those passwords again for a number of iterations.

At the bottom of the Account Policy dialog box is configuration information pertinent to unauthorized logon attempts. If these settings are configured (and they should be), Windows NT will lock out an account after a given number of bad logon attempts. In order to enable this, you must specify the number of bad attempts that will activate the lockout, how long the system should wait following a bad logon attempt before resetting the counter, and how long the account should stay locked out.

Here's a word of warning: If you choose Forever for the lockout duration, you are increasing the amount of work for the administrator, who must manually reset the account before the user can get back in again.

Auditing Changes to the User Account Database

When an organization implements decentralized administration of the Windows NT Account database, it may be desirable to audit all changes to the Accounts database. Remember, only members of the local groups Administrators and Account Operators can add, modify, and delete users in User Manager for Domains.

To enable auditing of changes to the account database, a member of the Administrators group must enable the auditing of User and Group Management, as shown in Figure 3.10. If the wish is to know exactly what files are being updated, File and Object Access should also be enabled.

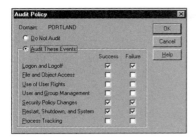

FIGURE 3.10
The Audit Policy dialog box.

At the risk of stating the obvious, File and Object Access is a two-step process. The first step was just described. After that, the administrator must enable the auditing of a particular file or directory from the security properties of the file or directory (as stands to reason, only files or directories on NTFS partitions may be audited).

The addition of File and Object access will help you determine when an Account Operator attempted to add a member to one of the Operator or Administrators local groups. When this attempt is made, that person sees a dialog box stating that his attempt was unsuccessful. Just auditing User and Group Management won't capture this error. You must enable File and Object Access so that you see the unsuccessful attempt to write to the SAM database.

System Policies

System policies help the network administrator restrict what configuration changes the user can perform to his profile. By combining roaming profiles and system policies, the administrator can give the user a consistent desktop and control what he can do to that desktop. Therefore, the administrator can be assured that the user can't modify certain settings.

System policies work very much like a merge operation. You can think of system policies as a copy of your Registry. When you log in to the network and the NTCONFIG.POL file exists on the domain controller, it will merge its settings into your Registry, changing your Registry settings as indicated in the system policy.

You implement system policies using the System Policy Editor, shown in Figure 3.11. It is automatically installed with any Windows NT Domain Controller. Select Start | Administrative Tools.

FIGURE 3.11
The System Policy Editor.

System policies can be configured to do the following:

- ◆ Implement defaults for hardware configuration for all computers using the profile or for a specific machine.

- ◆ Restrict the changing of specific parameters that affect the hardware configuration of the participating system.

- ◆ Set defaults for all users on the areas of their personal settings that they can configure.

- ◆ Restrict the user from changing specific areas of his configuration to prevent tampering with the system. An example would be disabling all Registry-editing tools for a specific user.

- ◆ Apply all defaults and restrictions on a group level rather than just a user level.

The System Policy Editor can also be used to change settings in the Registry of the system that System Policy Editor is being executed on. Many times, it's easier to use the System Policy Editor, because it has a better interface for finding common restrictions that you might want to place on a Windows NT Workstation.

Implementing System Policies

To create Computer, User, and Group policies, you must use the System Policy Editor. The System Policy Editor is automatically installed on all Domain Controllers and Member Servers and can be found under Start | Administrative Tools.

When you create a new policy file, you will see two default icons within the policy:

+ **Default Computer.** Used to configure all machine-specific settings. All property changes within this section will affect the HKEY_LOCAL_MACHINE subtree of the Registry. The Default Computer item will be used for any client that uses the policy and that doesn't have a specific machine entry created for itself in the policy file.

+ **Default User.** Used to specify default policy settings for all users who will be using the policy. The default user setting will affect the HKEY_CURRENT_USER subtree of the Registry. If the user is configured to use a roaming profile, this information will be stored in his centralized version of NTUSER.DAT in his profile directory.

Computer Policies

Computer policies can be configured to lock down common machine settings that will affect all users of a Windows NT system. Typically configured settings include the following:

+ Programs to automatically run at startup of the computer system. These can include virus scans. Opening the System/Run option in the Default Computer Properties sets this.

+ Ensuring that all Windows NT clients will have the administrative shares automatically created on startup of these systems. This enhances the administrator's ability to centrally manage the network. Opening the Windows NT Network/Sharing option in the Default Computer Properties sets this.

+ Implementing customized shared folders. These include the Desktop folder, the Start Menu folder, the Startup folder, and the Programs folder. These can be set to point to an actual network share location so that multiple machines can have common desktops or Start menus. Opening the Windows NT Shell/Custom shared folders option in the Default Computer Properties sets this.

+ Presenting a customized dialog box called the Logon Banner that can be used to inform users of upcoming maintenance to the network or for other network information. Opening the Windows NT System/Logon option in the Default Computer Properties sets this.

- Removing the last logged-on user from the Authentication dialog box. Because many users have poor passwords, knowing the user's login name can help someone guess that person's password. This is also set in the Windows NT System/Logon option in the Default Computer Properties.

Computer policies can also be implemented on a computer-by-computer basis. Selecting Edit | Add Computer accomplishes this. This will add a new icon to the policy with that computer's name.

User Policies

User policies can also be implemented through the system policy editor. These policies affect the HKEY_CURRENT_USER Registry subtree. Each user will be affected individually if a policy exists by his name. (Otherwise, the settings for Default User are active for him.)

User policies can also be implemented on a user-by-user basis. To create an individual user policy, select Edit | Add User. When a user logs in, NTCONFIG.POL will be checked to see if there is a policy for that user. If there isn't, the default user policy will be used for the login process.

Here are some common implementations of user profiles:

- Locking down display properties to prevent users from changing the resolution of their monitors. Display properties can be locked down as a whole or on each individual property page of display properties. This setting is adjusted in the Control Panel | Display | Restrict Display option of the Default User Properties sheet.

- Setting a default color scheme or wallpaper. This can be set in the Desktop option of the Default User Properties sheet.

- If you wish to restrict access to portions of the Start menu or Desktop, you can do so via the Shell | Restrictions option of the Default User Properties sheet.

- If you need to limit what applications can be run at a workstation, this can be set in the System | Restrictions option of the Default User Properties sheet. This option can also be used to prevent the user from modifying the Registry.

- You can prevent users from mapping or disconnecting network drives by setting the options in the Windows NT Shell | Restrictions option of the Default User Properties sheet.

Managing Disk Resources
At A Glance: Standard Permissions

Permission	Description
No Access	Restricts users from accessing the directory by any means.
List	Restricts users from accessing the directory, although they may view the directory's contents list.
Read	Users can read data files and execute program files from the directory but can't make changes.
Add	Users can't read or even view the contents of the directory, but they may write files to the directory.
Add & Read	Users may view and read from the directory and save new files to the directory, but they can't modify existing files.
Change	Users may view and read from the directory and save new files to the directory, they may modify and even delete existing files, and they may change attributes on the directory and even delete the entire directory.
Full Control	Users may view, read, save, modify, or delete the directory and its contents. In addition, users may change permissions on the directory and its contents, even if they don't own the resource. Users can also take ownership at any time.

Once your groups have been created in Windows NT, the next step of security is to protect your disk resources. Windows NT has two levels of security for protecting your disk resources:

- Share permissions

- NTFS permissions

The management of both sets of permissions will protect your Windows NT system from inappropriate access to your disk resources.

Creating and Sharing Resources

Share-level security allows a Windows NT administrator to protect his resources from network users. Not only do shares have a level of security, but they are also used as the entry point into the system for Windows NT network client users.

Four explicit share permissions can be implemented:

- **Read**. Allows a user to connect to the resource and run programs. He can also view any documents that are stored in the share, but he can't make any changes to them.

- **Change**. Allows a user to connect to a resource and run programs. It also allows him to create new documents and subfolders, modify existing documents, and delete documents.

- **Full Control**. Allows the user to do anything he wants in the share. It also allows him to change the share permissions to affect all users. The Full Control permission generally isn't required for most users. Change is sufficient for most day-to-day business needs.

- **No Access**. The most powerful permission. When it is implemented, the user who has been assigned this permission has no access to that resource. It doesn't matter what other permissions have been assigned. The No Access permission will override any other assigned permissions.

When a user, through group membership, has been assigned varying levels of share permissions, his effective shared permissions are the accumulation of his individual shared permissions.

The only time that this is not the case is when the user or a group that the user belongs to has been assigned the explicit permission of NO ACCESS. The NO ACCESS permission always takes precedence over any other permissions assigned.

Remember that local groups must be created in the Accounts database where the resource is located. If the resource is located on a domain controller, the local group can be created in the domain's Accounts database. If the resource is located on a Windows NT Workstation or a Windows NT Member Server, the local group must be created in that system's Accounts database.

Share permission can be set at only the root of a share, and all subdirectories of that share inherit the share's restrictions. For example, suppose a directory is shared as Users and given full control to the group Everyone. All subdirectories in the root of the share Users will have full control over the group Everyone. The only way to get around this problem is to either share at a lower level and implement security through lower-level shares or use NTFS security.

Implementing Permissions and Security
At A Glance: NTFS Permissions

Level	Directory Permissions	File Permissions
No Access	None	None
List	RX	Unspecified
Read	RX	RX
Add	WX	Unspecified
Add & Read	RXWD	RX
Change	RXWD	RXWD
Full Control	RXWDPO	RXWDPO

NTFS permissions allow you to assign more-comprehensive security to your computer system. NTFS permissions can protect you at the file level. Share permissions, on the other hand, can only be applied to the directory level. NTFS permissions can affect users logged on locally or across the network to the system where the NTFS permissions are applied. Share permissions are only in effect when the user connects to the resource via the network.

NTFS permissions, when applied at the directory level, can be applied as one of the default assignments listed in Table 3.1.

TABLE 3.1

NTFS DIRECTORY PERMISSIONS

NTFS Permission	Description
No Access (none) (none)	The user will have absolutely no access to the directory or its files. This will override any other NTFS permissions that the user might have assigned to him through other group memberships.
List (RX) (Not Specified)	Allows the user to view the contents of a directory and navigate to its subdirectories. It doesn't grant him access to the files in these directories unless this is specified in file permissions.
Read (RX) (RX)	Allows the user to navigate the entire directory structure, view the contents of the directory, view the contents of any files in the directory, and execute programs.

continues

TABLE 3.1 continued

NTFS Permission	Description
Add (WX) (Not Specified)	Allows the user to add new subdirectories and files to the directory. It doesn't give him access to the files within the directory unless specified in other NTFS permissions.
Add & Read (RWX) (RX)	Allows the user to add new files to the directory structure. Once a file has been added, the user has only read-only access to the files. This permission also allows the user to run programs.
Change (RWXD) (RWXD)	Allows the user to do the most data manipulation. He can view the contents of directories and files, run programs, modify the contents of data files, and delete files.
Full Control (All) (All)	Gives the user all of the abilities of the Change permission. In addition, the user can change the permissions on that directory or any of its contents. He can also take ownership of the directory or any of its contents.
Special Directory	Can be set as desired to any combination of (R)ead, (W)rite, E(X)ecute, (D)elete, Change (P)ermissions, and Take (O)wnership.

NTFS permissions can also be applied to individual files in directories. The NTFS file permissions are listed in Table 3.2.

TABLE 3.2

NTFS FILE PERMISSIONS

NTFS Permission	Description
No Access (none)	The user will have absolutely no access to that file. This will override any other NTFS directory and file permissions that may have been assigned to the user through other group memberships.
Read (RX)	Allows the user to view the contents of files but make no changes to the contents. The user can also execute the file if it is a program.
Change (RWXD)	Allows the user to make any editing changes he wants to a data file, including deleting the file.

NTFS Permission	*Description*
Full Control (All)	Gives the user all of the abilities of the Change permission. He can also change the permissions on that file and take ownership of that file if he isn't presently the owner.
Special File	Can be set as desired to any combination of (R)ead, (W)rite, E(X)ecute, (D)elete, Change (P)ermissions, and Take (O)wnership.

The determination of NTFS permissions is based on the cumulative NTFS permissions based on group membership. As with share permissions, the only wildcard is the No Access permission. If a user or a local group that the user belongs to is assigned the No Access permission, it doesn't matter what any other permissions assigned are. They will not have access.

Setting NTFS Permissions

NTFS permissions are set from the Security page of an NTFS file or directory object. To set NTFS permissions, a user must meet one of the following criteria:

- Be a member of the Administrators local group.

- Be a member of the Server Operators local group.

- Be a member of the Power Users local group in a Windows NT Workstation or Windows NT Member Server environment.

- Be assigned the NTFS permission of Change Permission (P) for a directory or file resource.

- Be the owner of a file or directory object. The owner of any object can change the permissions of that object at any time.

- Have the permission to Take Ownership so that he can become the owner of the file or directory object and change the permissions of that object.

Combining NTFS and Share Permissions

When combining NTFS and share permissions, remember the following tips:

- Users can be assigned only to global groups in the same domain.

- Only global groups from trusted domains can become members of local groups in trusting domains.

- NTFS permissions will be assigned only to local groups in all correct test answers.

- Only NTFS permissions will give you file-level security.

DISASTER RECOVERY

Various forms of disaster recovery can be implemented in a network, all the way from a good backup to a replicated site halfway across the country. For the Networking Essentials exam, Microsoft expects knowledge of backups, Uninterruptible Power Supplies, virus protection, and fault tolerance. Each of these categories is examined in the following sections.

Backups

Every network administrator should consider tape backups an important part of his job. A number of different strategies can be used in backing up files. One method is to copy a file to another drive. As in most operating systems, however, Windows 95, 98, and NT have special backup commands that help you maintain a systematic backup schedule.

Although backups can be accomplished by saving files to a different drive, they typically are performed with some form of tape drive (called DAT drives). Tape devices allow you to store several gigabytes and store them away from the system they backed up.

Microsoft identifies the following backup types:

- **Full backup**. Backs up all specified files.

- **Incremental backup**. Backs up only those files that have changed since the last backup.

- **Differential backup**. Backs up the specified files if the files have changed since the last full backup. This type doesn't mark the files as having been backed up.

Most backup plans use a combination of these backup types, such as a full backup once a week and an incremental or differential backup every other day of the week.

Full backups require a lengthy backup process each night, yet they make restoring simpler because there is only one set of tapes to deal with.

Incremental backups are much faster each night because there are fewer files to back up, yet restoring requires the administrator to restore the last full backup set, as well as all the incrementals performed since the drive failure.

Differential backups are similar to incrementals, except that they do not reset the Archive attribute, which means that each backup during the week backs up all files changed since the last full back-up. During a restoration, the administrator must restore the last full backup set as well as only the most recent differential set.

Uninterruptible Power Supplies

An Uninterruptible Power Supply (UPS) is a battery or generator that supplies power to an electronic device in the event of a power failure. UPSs commonly are used with network servers to prevent a disorderly shutdown by warning users to log out. After a predetermined period of time, the UPS software performs an orderly shutdown of the server. Many UPS units also regulate power distribution and serve as protection against power surges. Remember that a UPS generally doesn't provide for continued network functionality for longer than a few minutes. A UPS is not intended to keep the server running through a long power outage, but rather is designed to give the server time to do what it needs to do before shutting down. This can prevent the data loss and system corruption that sometimes results from sudden shutdown.

Prices run from the hundreds to many thousands of dollars. Before you buy, know how many servers you will be running off the UPS and how much time they need to shut down properly. One of the most popular UPS manufacturers is APC (American Power Conversion), a company that offers a full line of power supply and UPS products.

Virus Protection

On today's servers, virus protection is essential. One virus can be downloaded or installed from any file on a disk and can affect a single workstation. When that workstation interacts with the server, the virus can be uploaded to the workstation, where it can affect the server, as well as download itself to all other workstations that the server interacts with.

There are a number of excellent virus scanning/protection software packages on the market today, and every administrator should make certain there is at least a package on the server.

Fault Tolerance

Fault tolerance is defined as the ability to recover from a hardware failure. It is implemented and supported in Windows NT through the endorsement of RAID (Redundant Array of Inexpensive Disks). In addition to RAID 0 (the absence of fault tolerance), Windows NT supports RAID levels 1 and 5.

At A Glance: RAID

RAID Level	Implementation
0	Disk striping
1	Disk mirroring
5	Disk striping with parity

Implementing Disk Mirroring on Windows NT Server

Disk mirroring is the replication of data between two physical disks. When data comes in, it is written to both disks virtually simultaneously. If one disk fails, the system is able to stay up and running, since both disks have identical information on them. Only two actions can be performed: establishing the mirror, and breaking the mirror in the event of a hard drive failure. Both of these actions are performed in the Disk Administrator utility. With mirroring, two drives are controlled by one disk controller, and the cost of implementation is 50 percent of the available data space. (Two 2 GB drives give you a total data space of 4 GB, but when they are mirrored, you can store only 2 GB worth of data.)

Disk duplexing is a hardware enhancement over mirroring that doesn't involve any additional software interaction. In duplexing, two controllers are used instead of one. If one controller fails, the system can still stay up and running. This is still considered RAID 1 and is implemented as mirroring in Disk Administrator. With both mirroring and duplexing, read operations are performed quicker, because whichever disk isn't busy at the moment can process the request. Write requests are minimally slower, because data must be written twice rather than once.

To create a mirror using the Disk Administrator, follow these steps:

1. Select at least two areas of free space on different hard drives.

2. Choose Fault Tolerance, Establish Mirror.

The Disk Administrator then creates spaces of equal size on both disks and assigns a drive letter to them. The mirror set begins to duplicate all existing information from the first drive onto the mirror copy. Any new data is written to both drives by FTDISK.SYS.

Disk Striping with Parity

Disk striping with parity is RAID 5. With RAID 5, a minimum of three drives must be used, and a maximum of 32 can be used. An amount of free space on each drive is set aside as a portion of the set. When data comes in, it is written across all but one of the drives, and the last drive is used for a parity check on the data, which is written there. The drive chosen to hold the parity is different for each set of data written, so no one drive is reserved specifically for this purpose.

If any of the drives fail, the others can compute the missing data and recreate it. As with mirroring, Disk Administrator is used to implement disk striping with parity, through the command Create Stripe Set with Parity. If a drive fails and is replaced, the Regenerate command is used to place on the new drive the data that existed on the old.

Disk striping with parity slows system performance on both read and write requests, because multiple disks must always be accessed and parity always computed. Disk striping with parity can't be used on the system or boot partitions— they can be mirrored only.

To create a stripe set with parity, follow these steps:

1. Select between 3 and 32 areas of free disk space on each drive.

2. Choose Fault Tolerance, Create Stripe Set with Parity. You are prompted to enter the size of the set, with the default value being the maximum size available. (The minimum size is also shown for your information.)

3. In the Create Stripe Set with Parity dialog box, enter the size of the stripe set to create, and click OK.

The Disk Administrator calculates the total size of the stripe set with parity, based on the number of disks selected, and then creates a space that is equal on each disk. It then combines the drives into one logical volume.

As with anything else, you have to format the stripe set before it can be used. Save the changes by choosing Partition, Commit Changes Now, and then restart the system.

NETWORK ADAPTERS

Network adapter cards were discussed in passing in the preceding two chapters. Essentially, they are the item installed in the workstation (or server) to allow it to communicate across the cable with the network.

Most network adapter cards require a single interrupt in order to work, and there can be multiple cards within the same machine. With Windows 95 and 98, configuration of the card occurs automatically as a part of Plug and Play. With Windows NT, wizards walk you through the setup.

Here are common IRQ settings for a computer:

```
 0. System timer
 1. Keyboard
 2. Video card (EGA/VGA, and so on)
 3. COM 2 or 4
 4. COM 1 or 3
 5. Available
 6. Floppy disk
 7. LPT 1
 8. Real-time clock
 9. Available
10. Available
11. Available
12. PS/2 mouse
13. Math coprocessor
14. Hard disk
15. Available
```

Installing the card at an interrupt used by another device (such as a sound card or printer port) can cause a conflict.

NetBIOS Naming

NetBIOS (Network Basic Input/Output System) is an application interface that gives PC-based applications uniform access to lower protocol layers. Once considered an extension of the NetBEUI (NetBIOS Extended User Interface) protocol, it has outgrown NetBEUI and is now available with many protocol configurations, such as NetBIOS over IPX and NetBIOS over TCP/IP.

The major requirement of a NetBIOS network is that every computer must have a unique computer name that is 15 characters or less in length. The name can include alphanumeric characters and any of the following special characters:

! @ # $ % ^ & ( ) - _ ' { } . ~

The names are not case sensitive, and you can't use a space or an asterisk.

It is highly recommended that you use names that are descriptive and easily recognized for that machine. Here are some examples:

```
NANCY'S_PC
D_S_TECH_PC
TRNG_ROOM
```

With most Windows-based operating systems (95, 98, NT), you designate a computer name for the PC when you install the operating system. You can later change the computer name through the Control Panel Network application, but you must have Administrative privileges to do so.

To change the NetBIOS computer name in Windows NT, do the following:

1. Select Start | Settings | Control Panel.

2. Choose the Network applet.

3. From the Identification tab, click the Change button.

4. Change the computer name in the text box and click OK.

The Universal Naming Convention is a standard for identifying resources on Microsoft networks. A UNC path consists of the following components:

- A NetBIOS computer name preceded by a two backslashes
- The share name of a shared resource located on the given PC (optional)
- The MS-DOS-style path of a file or a directory located on the given share (optional)

Together, the items form an entry of the form *computername**sharename**path**file*.

Elements of the UNC path are separated by single backslashes. Many commands in Windows NT and Windows 95 and 98 use UNC paths to designate resources. Here are two examples:

```
net view \\D_S_TECH
net use Z: \\D_S_TECH\WRITING
```

You would use these commands to view the shared resources on that computer or to map the shared directory to drive Z.

MONITORING THE NETWORK

There are two major reasons to monitor a network. The first is to identify problems that exist and immediately begin trying to solve them. The second reason is to look for trends on the network that can identify excessive usage of a particular component. If a trend of this nature can be found, you can begin to plan for replacing or upgrading that component in the interest of speeding up your network.

"Trends" are identified through the use of *baselines*. A baseline is a collection of data that indicates how an individual system resource, a collection of system resources, or the system as a whole performs. This information is then compared to later activity to monitor system usage and system response to usage.

An established baseline allows you to compare system performance and see the deviations whenever any changes are made to the system. In the absence of a baseline, you can only guess at the results that changes make (good or bad).

Baselines or trends can be identified and isolated through hardware and software examination—both of which Performance Monitor can do. We will first look at how to create the baseline, and then we will look at Performance Monitor and other software tools.

Creating a Baseline

It's important to remember that, when setting up the baseline, you should carefully choose the resources to be monitored. Expect demands on a server to increase. Choose all the objects and counters that are important now and that you expect to be in the future. If objects aren't chosen in the initial baseline and then become important after the system is put into a production environment, there is nothing to compare data to.

Although all systems are unique (very few have identical hardware, software, and services installed), you should always include memory, processor, disk, and network objects in the baseline.

After the initial set of data is captured, use the same settings and capture data on a regular basis. Place this information in a database and analyze the system's performance. Has it become more efficient? Has it become slower? Are trends developing as more users, services, or applications are added to the server?

Hopefully, with a good set of data, you will be able to analyze a system and optimize its performance.

To create a baseline measurement, you must use the Log view. This is the only way to create a log of activity. While measuring, you will log, relog, and append logs to get a complete set of information.

As mentioned earlier, you should make an educated guess as to what should be selected before logging begins. Any kind of analysis should include the four basic objects mentioned earlier. When monitoring a server, however, you might want to include other objects, such as the following:

+ Cache

+ Logical disk

+ Memory

+ Network adapter

+ Network subnet activity on at least one server in the subnet

+ Physical disk (if using a RAID system)

+ Processor

+ Server

+ System

When relogging, increase the time interval to reduce the file size. In most cases, the extra data that is lost is not critical. As a rule of thumb, you might multiply the time interval by 10. For an initial time interval, you might use 60 seconds. Then, when relogging, use a time interval of 600 seconds. For most servers, this provides plenty of data.

Another option to consider is to append successive logs to the original log file. This way, all logs are kept together in a "master" log file or archive. No data is lost. To prevent confusion about where one set of data ends and another begins, bookmarks are automatically inserted to separate the logs.

Measurements should be taken for a full week at different times of the day so that information can be recorded at both peak and slack times each day. As is often mentioned, it is important to record activity during peak periods. It is also important to record activity during slack periods to see just what the level of activity is at those times. Ideally, you should have enough data to know whether there is any significant change in the different counters during different times of the day.

To automate the collection of data, Windows NT 4 can start Performance Monitor as a service. When started as a service, it has less impact on the system because there is no graphical display to use valuable resources. To use it as a service, use Performance Monitor to specify the data to be collected. Set the time interval to the desired frequency. Name the log file, and save the settings in a Performance Monitor workspace settings file. Configure Performance Monitor to start as a service when it reboots.

The second step in preparing for analysis is to take the collected data and put it into a database so that it can be analyzed. This involves collecting the information over a period of time and adding all of it to a database. Once in a database, the information can be used to identify bottlenecks and trends.

Bottlenecks are the problem areas that need addressing to improve the performance of the system, and trends are useful for capacity planning and preparing for future needs.

After the information is in a database, it is then accessible, measurable, and manageable. The database utilities complement the data-collection utilities. The collection utilities gather great quantities of data, and the database utilities allow you to organize the information into meaningful and manageable groups.

Numerous utilities can be used to analyze the data collected. Here are some that Microsoft provides:

- Performance Monitor
- Excel
- Access
- FoxPro
- SQL Server

In addition to these utilities, many other applications have been developed by other vendors.

Regardless of which application is used to analyze the data, the most important step is to collect the data over a significant period of time.

Performance Monitor

For the most part, Windows NT Server is self-tuning—one of the design goals that the Windows NT development team was striving for. An excellent utility, Performance Monitor, has been included with Windows NT Server to allow you to see how well your server and its components are running.

Performance Monitor is essentially the same utility that is included in Windows 95, where it is known as System Monitor. It divides components of the server into objects. An *object* represents individual threads, processes, physical devices, and sections of shared memory. Simply put, an object is a mechanism for identifying a system resource.

Objects are then further divided into counters, with each object having a unique set of counters assigned to it. In most cases, objects and their counters are available only when the computer is running the associated software or service. If the system is acting as a WINS server, for example, it has specific objects available that are not available on a non-WINS server. There is a set of common or core objects that can be monitored on any Windows NT 4 system. They are listed in Table 3.3.

TABLE 3.3

CORE OBJECTS CAPABLE OF BEING MONITORED

Name	Description
Cache	An area of physical memory that holds recently used data.
LogicalDisk	Partitions and other logical views of disk space.
Memory	Physical random access memory used to store code and data.
Objects	Certain system software objects.
Paging File	The file used to back up virtual memory locations to increase memory.
PhysicalDisk	A single spindle-disk unit or RAID device.
Process	A software object that represents a running program.
Processor	The hardware unit (CPU) that executes program instructions.
Redirector	The file system that diverts file requests to the network servers. It is also sometimes referred to as the Workstation service.
System	Contains counters that apply to all system hardware and software.
Thread	The part of a process that uses the processor.

When Performance Monitor is started, it begins in Chart view but is monitoring nothing. You must then select which objects you want to monitor and which counters to display.

To make your selections, do the following:

1. Click the Add Counter button on the toolbar, or select Edit | Add To Chart.

2. Select the object from the drop-down list.

3. Select the counter, or select Total for all instances.

To remove items from the chart, select a counter and press the Delete key.

After you choose what you want to view, the counters are visually displayed in graph (Chart) view. You can change from graph view to three other views:

- **Alert**. Allows you to configure intervals to sample an individual counter and alert you if thresholds are exceeded. Multiple alerts can be set at one time.

- **Log**. Allows you to log the information (store it in a file for future analysis). At any time, the log file can be opened in Performance Monitor and used to create any of the other three possibilities (a chart, a report, or an alert). When data is currently being logged, it can't be viewed from another view. If you try to open the log file, the log is stopped and the counter settings all are cleared.

- **Report**. Allows you to view the information statistically. It shows the value of the counter, and a report of all the counters can be created.

One key point to remember is that not all of the counters are available by default. Certain TCP/IP counters require the implementation of SNMP, and other networking counters require the use of Network Monitor Agent.

The PhysicalDisk object measures the performance of a physical disk, while the LogicalDisk object records parameters pertaining to a logical disk (a partition or logical drive that is identified by a drive letter).

PhysicalDisk Counters

The following counters are useful when you're looking for bottlenecks or problems related to the physical disk:

% Disk Time

% Disk Time reports the percentage of time that the physical disk was busy reading or writing.

Avg. Disk Queue Length

The average disk queue length is the average number of both read and write requests for a given disk.

LogicalDisk Counters

The following counters are useful when you're looking for bottlenecks or problems related to logical disks.

% Disk Time

% Disk Time reports the percentage of time that the logical disk C (or D) was busy. To monitor the total activity of all the partitions on a single disk drive, use the % Disk Time counter in Physical Disk.

Disk Queue Length

Disk Queue Length measures the number of read and write requests waiting for the logical disk to become available. Disk performance is suffering if this counter goes above 2.

The Processor Object

Many counters are associated with the processor object. In looking at them, however, be certain to remember that high levels of processor activity can result from two situations other than handling a processor-intensive task:

- A severe memory shortage in which the processor is busy managing virtual memory (swapping pages of memory to and from the disk).
- The system is busy handling a large number of interrupts.

In either of these cases, replacing the processor with a faster one doesn't address the real problem, so you must address the real cause.

% Processor Time

% Processor Time measures the time that the processor spent executing a non-idle thread—thus becoming the percentage of time that the processor was busy. The processor could be a bottleneck if the average value exceeds 80 percent.

Interrupts/sec

Interrupts/sec measures the number of interrupts that the processor handles per second. Hardware failures in I/O devices can be identified by an increase in the number of interrupts.

System: Processor Queue Length

System: Processor Queue Length measures the number of threads waiting in the queue for an available processor. A number routinely exceeding 2 can indicate a problem with processor performance.

The Memory Object

Symptoms of a memory shortage on a system include a busy processor and a high level of disk activity on the disk holding the page file. The former is indicative of managing virtual memory, while the latter is caused by accessing the disk to read and write memory pages.

Pages/sec

Pages/sec measures the number of times a memory page had to be paged in to memory or out to the disk. An increase in this value over time indicates an increase in paging activity.

Available Bytes

Available Bytes measures the amount of physical memory available. Excessive paging is seen when this value falls below 1 MB.

The Server Object

The Server component is responsible for handling all Server Message Block- (SMB) based requests for sessions, including file and print services.

If the Server service becomes the bottleneck, requests from clients are denied. This causes an ugly situation in which retries are forced and slower response times and increased traffic are the result.

Bytes Total/sec

Bytes Total/sec measures the number of bytes sent to and received from the network. It can be an overall indicator of how much information the Server service is handling.

Pool Nonpaged Failures and Pool Paged Failures

Pool Nonpaged Failures and Pool Paged Failures measure the number of times that a request from the server to allocate memory failed. Failures here indicate a memory shortage.

Remote Monitoring

Performance Monitor can be used to monitor computers other than the one on which you are working. Any computer configured to be remotely administered can be remotely monitored.

To select a remote computer to monitor, type the computer name in the Add Counter dialog box. The person doing the remote monitoring must be a member of the Administrators group of the target computer. In a Windows NT domain environment, the group Domain-Admins is always a member of each workstation's local Administrators group and can remotely monitor the system.

Network Monitor

Network Monitor is a tool that comes in a couple different formats. One format enables monitoring of the network traffic going in and out of the system running the monitor. A second format permits traffic to be monitored anywhere on the network. Windows NT 4 ships with the version that monitors only the system running the software, while Systems Management Server includes the Network Monitor that can monitor the entire network.

The advantage of the full version of Network Monitor is that any system can be monitored on the network. In addition, Network Monitor can be installed on machines running Windows for Workgroups, Windows 95, Windows NT Workstation, or Windows NT Server.

Network Monitor is made up of two components: the Network Monitor application and the Network Monitor Agent. The Network Monitor application lets a system capture and display network data, display network statistics, and save the captured data for future analysis.

The Network Monitor Agent, on the other hand, lets a computer capture all network traffic and send it over the network to the computer running the Network Monitor application. This capability is automatically installed on any computer running Network Monitor. It can be run on a Windows 95 system not running the Network Monitor application just to gather network traffic. The information that the Windows 95 system gathers can then be sent to a system running Network Monitor for viewing and analyzing the data. A Network Monitor Agent is available for both Windows 95 and Windows NT. The Network Monitor Agent can also be configured by setting capture and display passwords, as well as by specifying which network card will be monitored if there are multiple cards.

To install the simple version of Network Monitor, do the following:

1. Open Control Panel.

2. Click the Network icon to open the Network dialog box.

3. Select the Services tab and click Add.

4. Select Network Monitor Tools and Agent, and then click OK until you return to Control Panel.

Ways to Increase Optimization

There are a number of ways to increase the optimization of your system, based on what the potential bottleneck may be. Table 3.4 summarizes those that offer the greatest potential gain.

TABLE 3.4

OPTIMIZATION INCREASES

Item	Considerations
Processor	Upgrade the speed Add another processor Upgrade the secondary cache
Memory	Add more RAM Disable shadowing of ROM BIOS
Disk	Replace slow disks Use NTFS Defragment when necessary Upgrade from IDE to SCSI Isolate I/O-intensive tasks to separate disks Create a stripe set
Network	Get a faster network card Divide the network into multiple networks

Other considerations should include using hardware-based RAID solutions instead of software-based ones, optimizing the paging file, and optimizing the server service.

The recommended initial paging file size is equal to the amount of RAM plus 12 MB on NT Workstation and the amount of RAM on NT Server. The paging file should never be placed across a stripe set with parity. The paging file can be optimized in the Virtual Memory dialog box. To reach it, select Start | Settings | Control Panel, and click the System icon. Select the Performance tab, and click the Change button.

Keep in mind that the paging file can be spread across several disks if your hardware supports writing to those disks at the same time and the paging file can be moved to the disk with the lowest activity. In brief, if NT can access a hard disk, it can place a pagefile on it.

NOTE

Microsoft recommends placing the pagefile on a hard disk that doesn't house the Windows NT directory.

You optimize the server service by selecting the Services tab of the Network applet in Control Panel. Highlight Server and choose Properties. Arguably, no other change you can make on the server will have as dramatic an impact as this dialog box can.

WHAT IS IMPORTANT TO KNOW

The following list summarizes the chapter and accentuates the key concepts to memorize for the exam:

- Templates can be used to simplify the establishment of new user accounts.

- Permissions (user rights) for user accounts are kept in the user's access token, which is created only when the user logs in.

- For security reasons, Windows NT supports both local groups and global groups.

- Global groups exist across the domain.

- Local groups are local to the machine in question.

- Local groups are used to assign rights and permissions to a local system or local resource.

- Global groups are used to group user accounts within a single domain.

- Local groups can contain global groups.

- Global groups can't contain local groups.

- Performance Monitor is NT's all-around tool for monitoring a network using statistical measurements called counters.

- Performance Monitor can collect data on both hardware and software components, called objects. Its primary purpose is to establish a baseline from which everything can be judged.

- Every object has a number of counters. Some to be familiar with are those for the Paging File object—%Usage and %Usage Peak, which will tell if a paging file is reaching its maximum size.

- You *must* install the Network Monitor Agent to be able to see several of the network performance counters.

- To monitor a number of servers and be alerted if a counter exceeds a specified number, create one Performance Monitor alert for each server on your workstation.

OBJECTIVES

▶ Identify common errors associated with components required for communications.

▶ Diagnose and resolve common connectivity problems with cards, cables, and related hardware.

▶ Resolve broadcast storms.

▶ Identify and resolve network performance problems.

CHAPTER 4

Troubleshooting

IDENTIFYING COMMON ERRORS

Event Viewer, in Windows NT, is the first utility you should use in attempting to identify common errors. Windows NT includes the Event Viewer application in the Administrative Tools program group for viewing the messages stored in the system, security, and application log files.

System Log

The system log, the default view in Event Viewer, is maintained by the operating system. It tracks three kinds of events:

- **Errors**. These are symbolized by red stop signs. They indicate the failure of a Windows NT component or device, or perhaps an inability to start. These errors are common on notebook computers when Windows NT fails to start the network components because PCMCIA network cards are not present.

- **Warnings**. These are symbolized by exclamation points in a yellow circle. They indicate an impending problem. Low disk space on a partition triggers a warning, for example.

- **Information Events**. These are symbolized by an I in a blue circle. They indicate an event that isn't at all bad but is still somehow significant. Browser elections often cause information events.

Security Log

The security log remains empty until you enable auditing through User Manager. After you enable auditing, the audited events reside here. The security log tracks two types of events:

- **Success audits**. Symbolized by a key, these indicate successful security access.

- **Failure audits**. Symbolized by a padlock, these indicate unsuccessful security access.

Application Log

The application log collects messages from native Windows NT applications. If you aren't using any Win32 applications, this log remains empty—with the exception of many third-party applications that write their messages here as well.

Configuring Event Viewer

By default, log files can reach 512 KB, and events are overwritten after seven days. You can change these settings in the Event Log Settings dialog box, which you open by choosing Log | Log Settings from Event Viewer.

The Log | Save As menu option lets you save the log as either of the following:

♦ An event log file (with an EVT extension), making it available for examination on another computer at a future time

♦ A comma-separated value text file (with a TXT extension) for importing into a spreadsheet or database

Using Event Viewer

To find the source of the problem when services fail to start (or when they crash), look at the system log, under the Event heading. Somewhere toward the top of the column, you should find an Event code of 6005. By default, the logs list the most recent events at the top of the list, so start scanning from the top, or you might not find the most recent 6005 event. Event 6005 means that the EventLog service was successfully started.

To examine an event message, double-click an event to open the Event Detail dialog box.

Note the identifying information for the event:

♦ Date of the event

♦ Time of the event

- User account that generated the event, if applicable (usually found in the security log)

- Computer on which the event occurred

- Event ID (the Windows NT Event code)

- Source Windows NT component that generated the event

- Type of event (error, warning, and so on)

- Category of event (logon/logoff audit, for example)

- Description of the event

- Data in hexadecimal format (useful to a developer or debugger)

These are the items that constitute event messages.

Filtering Log Files

Log files can be of considerable size, and finding an individual event can be difficult unless you employ filtering. To filter the log, choose View | Filter. A dialog box appears, allowing you to specify a subset to view. Here are some of the different items you can filter on:

- **View From**. This lets you set the earliest date that you want to see.

- **View Through**. Sets the last date that you want to see.

- **Types**. The types of events that you want to be able to see.

- **Source**. The application, service, or driver that you want to see events for. This could be something like FTDISK or BROWSER.

- **Category**. The category of the error. In the system log, this is not normally used. In the security log, this is the area that you are auditing.

- **User**. Looks for errors that have this user name.

- **Computer**. Looks for errors that have this computer name.

- **Event ID**. Lists only the errors with this event ID.

When you want to go back to seeing all events, select View | All Events.

Searching for Events

To find an individual event, choose View | Find; the Find dialog box appears. The options in it are similar to the Filter Events dialog box, except that date fields are missing.

After specifying your criteria and pressing Enter, you will find the first occurrence in the list (the most recent). Pressing F3 moves you through the list. As you do so, you will see the errors in the order of their occurrence (from most recent to oldest).

CONNECTION PROBLEMS

Network problems are often caused by cabling, adapter IRQ conflicts, or problems with protocols. In general, you should use a diagnostics program to check the network adapter card, a cable analyzer to check the cabling, and Network Monitor (or a network protocol analyzer).

Cabling Problems

When working with networking cabling problems, check the following:

- Make sure that connector pins are correct and crimped tightly. Look for bent or broken pins.

- Make sure that all the component cables in a segment are connected. A user who moves his coaxial Ethernet client and removes the BNC T-connector incorrectly can cause a broken segment.

- Look for electrical interference (power cords, fluorescent lights, electric motors, and so on)

- On coaxial Ethernet LANs, look for missing terminators or improper impedance ratings. With 10BASE-T, make sure the cable used has the correct number of twists to meet the data-grade specifications. Watch out for malfunctioning transceivers, concentrators, and T-connectors.

Here are some tools that can be used in troubleshooting the physical network:

- **Digital Volt Meter.** Troubleshoots cabling problems by checking voltage and resistance.

- **Time-Domain Reflectors.** Send sound wave pulses through cable and look for breaks.

- **Oscilloscope.** An all-purpose tool for measuring signal voltage over time. It can be used to find shorts.

- **Protocol Analyzer.** Can be used to examine a packet and look for problems with the protocol itself (such as traffic, connections, errors, and so on).

- **Network Monitor.** Can dissect packets and look for errors, collisions, and traffic to and from individual computers.

Network Monitor

Windows NT Server 4 includes a tool called Network Monitor, which was mentioned briefly in Chapter 3, "Implementation." Network Monitor captures and filters packets and analyzes network activity. The Network Monitor included with Windows NT Server can monitor only the specific system on which it is installed, unlike the Network Monitor in Microsoft's Systems Management Server package, which can monitor other systems on the network.

Installing Network Monitor

To install Windows NT Server's Network Monitor, follow these steps:

1. Start the Network application in Control Panel.

2. Click the Services tab.

3. Click the Add button and select Network Monitor Tools and Agent from the network services list.

After Network Monitor is installed, it appears in the Administrative Tools program group.

Network Monitor Panes

The Network Monitor window is divided into four sections, or panes. The Graph pane (in the upper-left corner) shows the current network activity in a series of five bar charts. Note the scroll bar to the right of the Graph section. To view the bar charts, scroll down or drag the lower border down, exposing the hidden charts. The five bar graphs are as follows:

- % Network Utilization
- Frames Per Second
- Bytes Per Second
- Broadcasts Per Second
- Multicasts Per Second

Below the Graphs pane you see the Session Stats pane. It indicates the exchange of information from two nodes on the network, the amount of data, and the direction of travel. This data is limited to a per-session basis.

The Session Stats pane reports only on the first 128 sessions it finds. You can specify a particular session creating a capture filter.

The Session Stats pane collects information on the following four areas:

- **Network Address 1**. The first node included in a network session.
- **1 to 2**. The number of packets sent from the first address to the second.
- **2 to 1**. The number of packets sent from the second address to the first.
- **Network Address 2**. The second node included in the network session.

On the right side of the display windows is the Total Stats pane, which reveals information relevant to all the activity on the network. Whether statistics are supported depends on the network adapter. If a given network adapter isn't supported, Unsupported replaces the label.

The Total Stats information is divided into the following five categories:

Network Statistics

Total Frames
Total Broadcasts
Total Multicasts
Total Bytes
Total Frames Dropped
Network Status

Captured Statistics

Captured Frames
Captured Frames in Buffer
Captured Bytes
Capture Bytes in Buffer
%Buffer Utilized
#Frames Dropped

Per Second Statistics

% Network Utilization
#Frames/second
Bytes/second
Broadcasts/second
Multicasts/second

Network Card (MAC) Statistics

Total Frames
Total Broadcasts
Total Multicasts
Total Bytes

Network Card (MAC) Error Statistics

Total Cyclical Redundancy Check (CRC) Errors
Total Dropped Frames Due to Inadequate Buffer Space
Total Dropped Packets Due to Hardware Failure(s)

At the bottom of the display window, you see the Station Stats pane. It displays information specific to a workstation's activity on the network. You can sort on any category by right-clicking the column label.

The Station pane reports on only the first 128 sessions it finds. You can specify a particular session using a capture filter.

The following eight categories constitute the Station pane:

- Network Address
- Frames Sent
- Frames Rcvd
- Bytes Sent
- Bytes Rcvd
- Directed Frames Sent
- Multicasts Sent
- Broadcasts Sent

Adapter Conflicts

When working with network adapter card problems, check the following:

- Make sure that the cable is properly connected to the card and that you have the correct network adapter card driver.
- Make certain that the card is bound to the right transport protocol and that both are compatible with your operating system.
- Look for resource conflicts, making certain that another device isn't attempting to use the same resources.
- If there is a resource conflict, run the network adapter card's diagnostic software.
- Pull the card and reseat it, making certain that it fits properly in the slot.
- Replace the card with one that you know works. If the connection works with a different card, you know the card is the problem.

You can often isolate problems by pinging the other computers on your network. Here is a common diagnostic procedure:

1. Ping the 127.0.0.1 (the loopback address).

2. Ping your own IP address.

3. Ping the address of another computer on your subnet.

4. Ping the default gateway.

5. Ping a computer beyond the default gateway.

Check the Control Panel Services applet to ensure that the Server service and the Workstation service (and any other vital services that might affect connectivity) are running properly. Check the Bindings tab in the Control Panel Network applet to ensure that the services are bound to applications and adapters.

BROADCAST STORMS

A broadcast storm is a sudden flood of broadcast messages that clogs the transmission medium, approaching 100 percent of the bandwidth. Broadcast storms cause performance to decline and, in the worst case, computers can't even access the network. The cause of a broadcast storm is often a malfunctioning network adapter, but a broadcast storm can also be caused when a device on the network attempts to contact another device that either doesn't exist or doesn't respond to the broadcast for some reason.

If the broadcast messages are viable packets (or even error-filled but partially legible packets), a network-monitoring or protocol-analysis tool can often determine the source of the storm. If the broadcast storm is caused by a malfunctioning adapter throwing illegible packets onto the line, and a protocol analyzer can't find the source, try to isolate the offending PC by removing computers from the network one at a time until the line returns to normal.

TCP/IP-Related Problems

If you are using TCP/IP, the three main parameters that specify how TCP/IP is configured are as follows:

- The IP address (the network address and host address of the computer)

- The subnet mask, which specifies what portion of the IP address specifies the network address and what portion of the IP address specifies the host address

- The default gateway (most commonly, the address of the router)

Using a DHCP server can greatly reduce TCP/IP configuration problems. Scopes are ranges of available addresses on a DHCP server. The most important part of the configuration is to make sure you don't have duplicate addresses in the different scopes.

Utilities to use in TCP/IP-related troubleshooting include the following:

- ARP. This utility displays the Address Resolution Protocol cache of MAC addresses.

- IPCONFIG. Displays the IP configuration information for the host. Should be used with the /ALL parameter to see DNS, WINS, DHCP, and NetBIOS information.

- NBTSTAT. Shows NetBIOS-to-IP address mappings. NetBIOS names are cached as they are resolved.

- NETSTAT. Displays all the TCP/IP protocol statistics.

- NSLOOKUP. Displays DNS server entry information.

- PING. Used with either IP addresses or host names (if there is a method to resolve them to IP addresses) to verify that you can get to another host.

- ROUTE. Displays the routing table and lets you add entries with ROUTE ADD, or look at the table with ROUTE PRINT.

- TRACERT. An improvement over PING that traces the route being taken by the packet and displays the results.

NETWORK PERFORMANCE PROBLEMS

Performance Monitor, discussed in Chapter 3, is the primary tool included with Windows NT for monitoring the network's performance. Other items you should be aware of are discussed in the following sections.

Windows NT Boot Failures

The boot process begins when your computer accesses the hard drive's *Master Boot Record* (MBR) to load Windows NT. If your system fails during the *Power On Self Test* (POST), the problem isn't Windows NT-related; instead, it is a hardware issue. What happens after the MBR's program loads depends on the type of computer you're using.

Intel Boot Sequence

On Intel x86-based computers, the boot sector of the active partition loads a file called NTLDR. Similar to IO.SYS for MS-DOS or Windows 95, NTLDR is a hidden, system, read-only file in the root of your system partition. It's responsible for loading the rest of the operating system. NTLDR carries out the following steps:

1. It switches the processor to the 32-bit flat memory model necessary to address 4 GB of RAM.

2. It starts the minifile system driver necessary for accessing the system and boot partitions. This minifile system driver contains just enough code to read files at boot time. The full file systems are loaded later.

3. NTLDR displays a Boot Loader menu that gives the user a choice of operating system to load, and then waits for a response. The options for the Boot Loader menu are stored in a system, read-only file named BOOT.INI that is in the root of your system partition.

4. If Windows NT is the selected system, NTLDR invokes the hardware-detection routine to determine the hardware required. NTDETECT.COM (the same program that detects the hardware during NTSETUP) performs the hardware detection, builds the hardware list, and returns it to NTLDR. NTDETECT.COM is hidden, system, and read-only in the root of the system partition.

5. NTLDR loads the kernel of the operating system. The kernel is called NTOSKRNL.EXE, and you can find it in the <winnt_root>\SYSTEM32 directory. At this point, the screen clears and displays OS Loader version 4.00.

6. NTLDR loads the Hardware Abstraction Layer (HAL). The HAL is a single file (HAL.DLL) that contains the code necessary to mask interrupts and exceptions from the kernel.

7. It loads SYSTEM, the HKEY_LOCAL_MACHINE\SYSTEM hive in the Registry. You can find the corresponding file in the <winnt_root>\SYSTEM32\CONFIG directory.

8. NTLDR loads the boot-time drivers. Boot-time drivers have a start value of 0. These values are loaded in the order in which they are listed in HKEY_LOCAL_MACHINE\SYSTEM\CurrentControlSet\Control\ ServiceGroupOrder. Each time a driver loads, a dot is added to the series following the OS Loader V4.00 at the top of the screen. If the /sos switch is used in BOOT.INI, the name of each driver appears on a separate line as each is loaded. The drivers are not initialized yet.

9. NTLDR passes control, along with the hardware list collected by NTDETECT.COM, to NTOSKRNL.EXE.

After NTOSKRNL.EXE takes control, the boot phase ends and the load phases begin.

RISC Boot Sequence

On a RISC-based computer, the boot process is much simpler, because the firmware does much of the work that NTLDR and company do on the Intel platform. RISC-based computers maintain hardware configuration in their firmware (also called nonvolatile RAM), so they don't need NTDETECT.COM. Their firmware also contains a list of valid operating systems and their locations, so they don't need BOOT.INI either.

RISC-based machines don't look for the Intel-specific NTLDR to boot the operating system; instead, they always look for a file called OSLOADER.EXE. This file is handed the hardware configuration data from the firmware. It then loads NTOSKRNL.EXE, HAL.DLL, and SYSTEM, and the boot process concludes.

Booting to Windows 95, MS-DOS, or OS/2

On Intel-based computers, you can install Windows NT over Windows 95 or MS-DOS. The boot loader screen offers the user a choice of Windows NT Server 4, Microsoft Windows, or MS-DOS. If the user chooses a non-Windows NT operating system, a file called BOOT-SECT.DOS is loaded and executed. BOOTSECT.DOS is a hidden, system, read-only file in the root of the system partition. It contains the information that was present in the boot sector before Windows NT was installed. If the user chooses Windows 95 from the boot menu, for example, BOOTSECT.DOS loads IO.SYS and passes control to it.

BOOT.INI

Because not all machines use MS-DOS-style paths (for example, c:\winnt) to refer to locations on a hard drive, Windows NT uses a cross-platform standard format called Advanced RISC Computer (ARC) within BOOT.INI. An ARC-compliant path consists of four parameters:

Parameter	Description
`scsi(x)` or `multi(x)`	Identifies the hardware adapter
`disk(y)`	SCSI bus number; always 0 if multi
`rdisk(z)`	Physical drive number for multi; ignored for SCSI
`partition`	Logical partition number

The first three parameters are 0-based; that is, the first physical IDE drive is `rdisk(0)` and the second is `rdisk(1)`. The partition parameter, however, is 1-based, so the first partition on the drive is `rdisk(0)partition(1)`.

All of the parameters—even the ones that are ignored—must be present in the path. For instance, `multi(0)disk(0)rdisk(0)partition(1)` is a valid path even though `disk(0)` is essentially unnecessary. `multi(0)rdisk(0)partition(1)` is not valid.

The first parameter almost always is multi, even for a SCSI controller. The only time you even see SCSI in a BOOT.INI file is if the BIOS on the controller is turned off. If this is the case, don't worry; an additional hidden, system, read-only file, NTBOOTDD.SYS, is present in the root of the system partition. NTBOOTDD.SYS is a device driver necessary for accessing a SCSI controller that doesn't have an on-board BIOS or that doesn't use INT 13 to identify hard disks. If this file is present, you'll probably see a scsi(x) entry in BOOT.INI. If you don't, you probably upgraded from Windows NT 3.1 (where this setting was more common) without ever deleting the file.

The same holds true for a RISC-based computer: If you look at the firmware entries for the operating system paths, you should see the same kind of ARC-compliant paths.

Boot Components

NTLDR may invoke the Boot Loader menu, but BOOT.INI, an editable text file, controls it. (It is read-only, so you must remove that attribute before editing it.) BOOT.INI is the only INI file that Windows NT uses—if, indeed, you can actually say that Windows NT uses it. After all, Windows NT is not loaded when this file is called on.

BOOT.INI has only two sections: [boot loader] and [operating systems].

The [boot loader] section of BOOT.INI specifies the operating system that will be loaded if the user doesn't make a selection within a defined period of time. By default, you see something like this:

```
[boot loader]
timeout=30
default=multi(0)disk(0)rdisk(0)partition(1)\WINNT
```

The timeout parameter is the length of time (in seconds) that NTLDR has to wait for the user to make a decision. If timeout is set to 0, the default operating system loads immediately. If it is set to -1, the menu displays until the user makes a decision.

The default parameter defines the actual path to the directory that contains the files for the default operating system.

You can edit BOOT.INI directly, but remember that a mistyped character in NOTEPAD.EXE or EDIT.COM could result in your system's not booting properly.

The [operating systems] section contains a reference for every operating system available to the user from the Boot Loader menu, as well as any special switches necessary to customize the Windows NT environment. One of these entries must match the default= entry in the [boot loader] section. Otherwise, you end up with two entries for the same OS on-screen, one of which has "(default)" following it.

Note that the paths are in ARC format with a label in quotation marks, which displays as an on-screen selection. Here's an example of an [operating systems] section:

```
multi(0)disk(0)rdisk(0)partition(1)\WINNT=
```

The following list delineates several useful switches that you can include in the [operating systems] section of BOOT.INI. The only way to include them is to manually edit the BOOT.INI file (take the read-only attribute off first and save the file as a text file):

- /basevideo. Tells Windows NT to load the standard VGA driver rather than the optimized driver written for your video card. This is useful, for example, if your monitor breaks and is replaced by one that doesn't support the resolution or refresh rate that your last one did. Selecting the VGA mode entry uses the standard VGA 640X480 16-color driver that works with almost every monitor.

- /sos. Enumerates to the screen each driver as it loads during the kernel load phase. If Windows NT hangs during this phase, you can use the /sos switch to determine which driver caused the problem.

> **NOTE**
> When NT is booted by using the option Windows NT Server Version 4.00 [VGA mode], both /sos and /basevideo are used.

- /noserialmice=[COMx¦COMx,y,z_]. When Windows NT boots, NTDETECT.COM looks for, among other things, the presence of serial mice. Sometimes this detection routine misfires and identifies modems or other devices as serial mice. Then, when Windows NT loads and initializes, the serial port is unavailable and the device is unusable because Windows NT is expecting a serial mouse. In other instances, the serial mouse detection signal can shut down a UPS connected to the serial port. The /noserialmice switch by itself tells NTDETECT.COM not to bother looking for serial mice. Used with specific COM port(s), NTDETECT.COM still looks for serial mice, but not on the port(s) specified.

- /crashdebug. Turns on the Automatic Recovery and Restart capability, which you can also configure using the Control Panel System application. In fact, when you configure this capability through

Control Panel, what you are doing is merely adding this switch to the OS path in BOOT.INI.

◆ /nodebug. Programmers often use a special version of Windows NT that includes debugging symbols that are useful for tracking down problems with code. This version of Windows NT runs slowly compared to the retail version, owing to the extra overhead in tracking every piece of executing code. To turn off the monitoring in this version of Windows NT, add the /nodebug switch to the OS path in BOOT.INI.

◆ /maxmem:n. Memory parity errors can be notoriously difficult to isolate. The /maxmem switch helps. When followed by a numeric value, this switch limits Windows NT's usable memory to the amount specified in the switch. This switch is also useful for developers using high-level workstations who want to simulate performance on a lower-level machine.

◆ /scsiordinal:n. If your system has two identical SCSI controllers, you need a way to distinguish one from the other. The /scsiordinal switch is used to assign a value of 0 to the first controller and 1 to the second.

Kernel Initialization Phase

After all the initial drivers have loaded, the screen turns blue and the text height shrinks; the kernel initialization phase has begun. Now the kernel and all the drivers loaded in the previous phase are initialized. The Registry begins to flesh out. The CurrentControlSet is copied to the CloneControlSet, and the volatile HARDWARE key is created. The system Registry hive is then scanned once more for higher-level drivers configured to start during system initialization.

Services Load Phase

Here the session manager scans the system hive for a list of programs that must run before Windows NT fully initializes. These programs may include AUTOCHK.EXE, the boot-time version of CHKDSK.EXE that examines and repairs any problems within a file system, or AUTO-CONV.EXE, which converts a partition from FAT to NTFS. These boot-time programs are stored in the following:

```
HKEY_LOCAL_MACHINE\SYSTEM\CurrentControlSet\Control\
```

Following these programs, the page file(s) are created based on the locations specified in

```
HKEY_LOCAL_MACHINE\SYSTEM\CurrentControlSet\Control\
```

Next, the SOFTWARE hive loads from <winnt_root>\SYSTEM32\ CONFIG. Session Manager then loads the CSR subsystem and any other required subsystems from

```
HKEY_LOCAL_MACHINE\System\CurrentControlSet\Control\
```

Finally, drivers that have a start value of 2 (Automatic) load.

Windows Start Phase

After the Win32 subsystem starts, the screen switches into GUI mode. The Winlogon process is invoked, and the Welcome dialog box appears. Although users can go ahead and log on at this point, the system might not respond for a few moments while the Service Controller initializes automatic services.

The critical file at this point is SERVICES.EXE, which actually starts Alerter, Computer Browser, EventLog, Messenger, NetLogon, Windows NT LM Security Support Provider, Server, TCP/IP NetBIOS Helper, and Workstation. A missing or corrupt SERVICES.EXE cripples your Windows NT-based computer.

After a user successfully logs on to the system, the LastKnownGood control set is updated and the boot is considered good. Until a user logs on for the first time, though, the boot/load process technically remains unfinished, so a problem that Windows NT can't detect but that a user can see (such as a video problem) can be resolved by falling back on the LastKnownGood configuration.

Control Sets and LastKnownGood

A control set is a collection of configuration information used during boot-up by Windows NT. A special control set called LastKnownGood plays a special role in troubleshooting the boot process.

After the system boots and a user logs on successfully, the current configuration settings are copied to the LastKnownGood control set in the Registry. These settings are preserved so that if the system can't boot successfully the next time a user attempts to log on, the system can fall back on LastKnownGood, which, as the name implies, is the last configuration known to facilitate a "good" boot. LastKnownGood is stored in the Registry under

```
HKEY_LOCAL_MACHINE\SYSTEM\CurrentControlSet
```

The key to understanding LastKnownGood lies in recognizing that it updates the first time a user logs on to Windows NT after a reboot.

To boot with the LastKnownGood configuration, press the spacebar when prompted during the boot process. You see the Hardware Profile/Configuration Recovery menu. Select a hardware profile and press L for the LastKnownGood configuration.

Windows NT will occasionally automatically boot using LastKnownGood, but only if the normal boot process produces severe or critical errors in loading device drivers.

LastKnownGood doesn't do you any good if files are corrupted or missing. You must use the Emergency Repair Process for help with that.

Troubleshooting RAS

If RAS isn't working, check the Event Viewer. Several RAS events appear in the system log. The first step in diagnosing RAS problems is often to turn on the DEVICE.LOG file, via editing the Registry. Once enabled, the log file is stored in \WINNT_ROOT\SYSTEM32\RAS.

You might also check the Control Panel Dial-Up Networking Monitor application. The Status tab of the Dial-Up Networking Monitor displays statistics on current conditions, including connection statistics and device errors.

RAS supports TCP/IP, NWLink, and NetBEUI protocols for both dial-in and dial-out connections. TCP/IP benefits from being available on a number of different platforms from being easily routable, and the compatibility choice of the Internet.

If you're having problems with PPP, you can log PPP debugging information to a file called PPP.Log in the \<winnt_root>\System32\Ras directory. To log PPP debugging information to PPP.Log, change the Registry value for the following subkey to 1:

```
\HKEY_LOCAL_MACHINE\System\CurrentControlSet\Services\
```

Microsoft has identified the following common RAS problems and some possible solutions:

- **Authentication**. RAS authentication problems often stem from incompatible encryption methods. Try to connect using the Allow any authentication including clear text option. If you can connect using clear text and you can't connect using encryption, you know that the client and server encryption methods are incompatible.

- **Callback with Multilink**. If a client makes a connection using Multilink over multiple phone lines, with Callback enabled, the server will call back using only a single phone line (in other words, Multilink functionality is lost). RAS can use only one phone number for callback. If the Multilink connection uses two channels over an ISDN line, the server can still use Multilink on the callback.

- **AutoDial at logon**. At logon, when Explorer is initializing, it might reference a shortcut or some other target that requires an AutoDial connection, causing AutoDial to spontaneously dial a remote connection during logon. The only way to prevent this is to disable AutoDial or to eliminate the shortcut or other target causing the AutoDial to occur.

Windows NT Diagnostics

Windows NT Diagnostics provides a tidy front end to much of the information in the HKEY_LOCAL_MACHINE Registry subtree. Like its ancestor, MSD from Windows 3.1, Windows NT Diagnostics can create incredibly detailed and valuable system configuration reports. One thing you can't do with Windows NT Diagnostics is edit the system configuration.

The Windows NT Diagnostics dialog box includes the following nine tabs:

- **Version**. Displays information stored under HKEY_LOCAL_MACHINE\ Software\Microsoft\Windows NT\CurrentVersion, including the build number, registered owner, and Service Pack update information.

- **System**. Displays information stored under HKEY_LOCAL_MACHINE\ Hardware, including CPU and other device identification information.

- **Display**. Displays information on the video adapter and adapter settings.

- **Drives**. Lists all drive letters in use and their types, including drive letters for floppy drives, hard disks, CD-ROM and optical drives, and network connections. Double-click a drive letter to display a drive properties dialog box. The General tab of the drive properties dialog box shows byte and cluster information for the drive, while the File System tab shows file system information.

- **Memory**. Displays the current memory load, as well as physical and virtual memory statistics.

- **Services**. Displays service information stored under HKEY_LOCAL_ MACHINE\System\CurrentControlSet\Services, including status. Click the Devices button to display driver information stored under HKEY_LOCAL_MACHINE\System\CurrentControlSet\Control, including status.

- **Resources**. Displays device information listed by interrupt and port, and also by DMA channels and UMB locations in use.

- **Environment**. Displays environment variables for command prompt sessions (set under Control Panel System).

- **Network**. Displays network component configuration and status.

WHAT IS IMPORTANT TO KNOW

The following list summarizes the chapter and accentuates the key concepts to memorize for the exam:

♦ The NT System log contains information about services and drivers that fail to start.

♦ You examine the System log with Event Viewer.

♦ When you're looking at a number of Stop errors in the system log via Event Viewer, the Stop error at the bottom of the list is generally the cause of all the others, because entries are written to the top of the file as they occur, and the other services can be dependent on the service that erred.

♦ The three main parameters that specify how TCP/IP is configured are

  · The IP address (the computer's network address and host address).

  · The subnet mask (specifies what portion of the IP address specifies the network address and what portion of the IP address specifies the host address).

  · The default gateway (most commonly, the address of the router).

♦ Using a DHCP server can greatly reduce TCP/IP configuration problems.

♦ Utilities to use in TCP/IP-related troubleshooting are

  · ARP. This utility displays the Address Resolution Protocol cache of MAC addresses.

  · IPCONFIG. Displays the IP configuration information for the host. Should be used with the /ALL parameter to see DNS, WINS, DHCP, and NetBIOS information.

  · NETSTAT. Displays all the TCP/IP protocol statistics.

  · NBTSTAT. Shows NetBIOS-to-IP address mappings. NetBIOS names are cached as they are resolved.

  · NSLOOKUP. Displays DNS server entry information.

  · PING. Used with either IP addresses or host names (if there is a method to resolve them to IP addresses) to verify that you can get to another host.

  · ROUTE. Displays the routing table and lets you add entries with ROUTE ADD or look at the table with ROUTE PRINT.

  · TRACERT. An improvement over PING that traces the route being taken by the packet and displays the results.

- Tools that can be used in troubleshooting the physical network include the following:

  - Digital Volt Meter. Troubleshoots cabling problems by checking voltage and resistance.

  - Network Monitor. Can dissect packets and look for errors, collisions, and traffic to and from individual computers.

  - Oscilloscope. An all-purpose tool for measuring signal voltage over time. It can be used to find shorts.

  - Protocol Analyzer. Can be used to examine a packet and look for problems with the protocol itself (such as traffic, connections, errors, and so on).

  - Time-Domain Reflectors. Send sound wave pulses through cable and look for breaks.

- When working with networking cabling problems, check the following:

  - Make sure that connector pins are correct and crimped tightly. Look for bent or broken pins.

  - Make sure that all the component cables in a segment are connected. A user who moves his coaxial Ethernet client and removes the BNC T-connector incorrectly can cause a broken segment.

  - Look for electrical interference—power cords, fluorescent lights, electric motors, and so on.

  - On coaxial Ethernet LANs, look for missing terminators or improper impedance ratings. With 10BASE-T, make sure that the cable used has the correct number of twists to meet the data-grade specifications. Watch out for malfunctioning transceivers, concentrators, and T-connectors.

- When working with network adapter card problems, check the following:

  - Make sure the cable is properly connected to the card and that you have the correct network adapter card driver.

  - Make certain that the card is bound to the right transport protocol and that both are compatible with your operating system.

  - Look for resource conflicts, making certain that another device isn't attempting to use the same resources.

  - If there is a resource conflict, run the network adapter card's diagnostic software.

  - Pull the card and reseat it, making certain that it fits properly in the slot.

  - Replace the card with one that you know works. If the connection works with a different card, you know the card is the problem.

The following section of Objective Review Notes is provided so you can personalize this book to maximum effect. This is your workbook, study sheet, notes section, whatever you want to call it. YOU will ultimately decide exactly what information you'll need, but there's no reason this information should be written down somewhere else. As the author has learned from his teaching experiences, there's absolutely no substitute for taking copious notes and using them *throughout* the study process.

There's a separate section—two to a page—for each subobjective covered in the book. Each subobjective section falls under the main exam objective category, just as you'd expect to find it. It is strongly suggested that you review each subobjective and immediately make note of your knowledge level; then return to the Objective Review Notes section repeatedly and document your progress. Your ultimate goal should be to be able to review this section alone and know if you are ready for the exam.

OBJECTIVE REVIEW NOTES

Suggested use:

1. Read the objective. Refer to the part of the book where it's covered. Then ask yourself the following questions:

    • Do you already know this material? Then check "Got it!" and make a note of the date.

    • Do you need some brushing up on the objective area? Check "Review it!" and make a note of the date. While you're at it, write down the page numbers you just checked, because you'll need to return to that section.

    • Is this material something you're largely unfamiliar with? Check the "Help!" box and write down the date. Now you can get to work.

2. You get the idea. Keep working through the material in this book and in the other study material you probably have. The better you understand the material, the quicker you can update and upgrade each objective notes section from "Help!" to "Review it!" to "Got it!".

3. Cross-reference the materials YOU are using. Most people who take certification exams use more than one resource at a time. Write down the page numbers of where this material is covered in other books you're using, or which software program and file this material is covered on, or which video tape (and counter number) it's on, or whatever you need that works for you.

Standards and Terminology

► Objective: Define common networking terms for LANs and WANs.

☐ **Got it!**
Date:_____

☐ **Review it!**
Date:_____

☐ **Help!**
Date:_____

Notes:

_____
_____
_____
_____
_____

Fast Track cross-reference, see pages:

_____
_____

Other resources cross-reference, see pages:

_____
_____
_____
_____

► Objective: Compare a file-and-print server with an application server.

☐ **Got it!**
Date:_____

☐ **Review it!**
Date:_____

☐ **Help!**
Date:_____

Notes:

_____
_____
_____
_____
_____

Fast Track cross-reference, see pages:

_____
_____

Other resources cross-reference, see pages:

_____
_____
_____

OBJECTIVE REVIEW NOTES

OBJECTIVE REVIEW NOTES

► Objective: Compare user-level security with access permission assigned to a shared directory on a server.

☐ **Got it!**
*Date:*_____

☐ **Review it!**
*Date:*_____

☐ **Help!**
*Date:*_____

Notes:
_____
_____
_____
_____
_____

Fast Track cross-reference, see pages:
_____
_____

Other resources cross-reference, see pages:
_____
_____
_____

► Objective: Compare a client/server network with a peer-to-peer network.

☐ **Got it!**
*Date:*_____

☐ **Review it!**
*Date:*_____

☐ **Help!**
*Date:*_____

Notes:
_____
_____
_____
_____
_____

Fast Track cross-reference, see pages:
_____
_____

Other resources cross-reference, see pages:
_____
_____
_____

► Objective: Compare the implications of using connection-related communications with connectionless communications.

☐ **Got it!**
  *Date:*_____

☐ **Review it!**
  *Date:*_____

☐ **Help!**
  *Date:*_____

Notes:

_____
_____
_____
_____
_____
_____

Fast Track cross-reference, see pages:

_____
_____

Other resources cross-reference, see pages:

_____
_____
_____

► Objective: Distinguish whether SLIP or PPP is used as the communications protocol in various situations.

☐ **Got it!**
  *Date:*_____

☐ **Review it!**
  *Date:*_____

☐ **Help!**
  *Date:*_____

Notes:

_____
_____
_____
_____
_____

Fast Track cross-reference, see pages:

_____

Other resources cross-reference, see pages:

_____
_____
_____

OBJECTIVE REVIEW NOTES

Objective: Define the communication devices that communicate at each level of the OSI model.

☐ **Got it!**
Date:_____

☐ **Review it!**
Date:_____

☐ **Help!**
Date:_____

Notes:
_____
_____
_____
_____
_____

Fast Track cross-reference, see pages:
_____

Other resources cross-reference, see pages:
_____
_____
_____
_____

Objective: Describe the characteristics and purpose of the media used in IEEE 802.3 and IEEE 802.5 standards.

☐ **Got it!**
Date:_____

☐ **Review it!**
Date:_____

☐ **Help!**
Date:_____

Notes:
_____
_____
_____
_____
_____

Fast Track cross-reference, see pages:
_____

Other resources cross-reference, see pages:
_____
_____
_____

OBJECTIVE REVIEW NOTES

► Objective: Explain the purpose of NDIS and Novell ODI network standards.

☐ Got it!
*Date:*_____

☐ Review it!
*Date:*_____

☐ Help!
*Date:*_____

Notes:

_____

_____

_____

_____

_____

_____

_____

Fast Track cross-reference, see pages:

_____

_____

_____

Other resources cross-reference, see pages:

_____

_____

_____

_____

_____

OBJECTIVE REVIEW NOTES

Planning

► Objective: Select the appropriate medium for various situations.

☐ Got it!   ☐ Review it!   ☐ Help!
*Date:*_____   *Date:*_____   *Date:*_____

Notes:

_____
_____
_____
_____
_____
_____
_____
_____
_____
_____
_____
_____
_____
_____
_____

Fast Track cross-reference, see pages:

_____
_____
_____

Other resources cross-reference, see pages:

_____
_____
_____
_____
_____

OBJECTIVE REVIEW NOTES

► Objective: Situational elements.

☐ **Got it!**
*Date:*_____

☐ **Review it!**
*Date:*_____

☐ **Help!**
*Date:*_____

Notes:

_____
_____
_____
_____
_____

Fast Track cross-reference, see pages:

_____
_____
_____

Other resources cross-reference, see pages:

_____
_____
_____
_____

► Objective: Select the appropriate technology for various token-ring and Ethernet networks.

☐ **Got it!**
*Date:*_____

☐ **Review it!**
*Date:*_____

☐ **Help!**
*Date:*_____

Notes:

_____
_____
_____
_____
_____

Fast Track cross-reference, see pages:

_____
_____

Other resources cross-reference, see pages:

_____
_____
_____

OBJECTIVE REVIEW NOTES

► Objective: Select the appropriate network and transport protocol or protocols for various token-ring and Ethernet networks.

☐ **Got it!**
Date:_____

☐ **Review it!**
Date:_____

☐ **Help!**
Date:_____

Notes:

_____
_____
_____
_____
_____
_____
_____
_____
_____
_____
_____
_____
_____
_____

Fast Track cross-reference, see pages:

_____
_____
_____
_____

Other resources cross-reference, see pages:

_____
_____
_____
_____
_____
_____

OBJECTIVE REVIEW NOTES

► Objective: Select the appropriate connectivity devices for various token-ring and Ethernet networks.

☐ **Got it!**
   Date:
☐ **Review it!**
   Date:
☐ **Help!**
   Date:

Notes:

_____

_____

_____

_____

_____

_____

_____

_____

_____

_____

_____

Fast Track cross-reference, see pages:

_____

_____

_____

_____

Other resources cross-reference, see pages:

_____

_____

_____

_____

_____

_____

OBJECTIVE REVIEW NOTES

► Objective: List the characteristics, requirements, and appropriate situations for WAN connection services.

☐ **Got it!**
Date:_____

☐ **Review it!**
Date:_____

☐ **Help!**
Date:_____

Notes:

_____
_____
_____
_____
_____
_____
_____
_____
_____
_____

Fast Track cross-reference, see pages:

_____
_____
_____
_____

Other resources cross-reference, see pages:

_____
_____
_____
_____
_____
_____
_____
_____

OBJECTIVE REVIEW NOTES

Implementation

▶ Objective: Choose an administrative plan to meet specified needs, including performance management, account management, and security.

☐ Got it!   ☐ Review it!   ☐ Help!
Date:_____   Date:_____   Date:_____

Notes:

_____
_____
_____
_____
_____

Fast Track cross-reference, see pages:

_____
_____

Other resources cross-reference, see pages:

_____
_____
_____
_____

▶ Objective: Choose a disaster recovery plan for various situations.

☐ Got it!   ☐ Review it!   ☐ Help!
Date:_____   Date:_____   Date:_____

Notes:

_____
_____
_____
_____
_____
_____

Fast Track cross-reference, see pages:

_____
_____

Other resources cross-reference, see pages:

_____
_____
_____

OBJECTIVE REVIEW NOTES

► Objective: Given the manufacturer's documentation for the network adapter, install, configure, and resolve hardware conflicts for multiple network adapters in a token-ring or Ethernet network.

☐ **Got it!**   ☐ **Review it!**   ☐ **Help!**
    Date: *Date:*   *Date:*

Notes:
_____
_____
_____
_____
_____

Fast Track cross-reference, see pages:
_____
_____

Other resources cross-reference, see pages:
_____
_____
_____

► Objective: Implement a NetBIOS naming scheme for all computers on a given network.

☐ **Got it!**   ☐ **Review it!**   ☐ **Help!**
    Date: *Date:*   *Date:*

Notes:
_____
_____
_____
_____
_____
_____

Fast Track cross-reference, see pages:
_____
_____

Other resources cross-reference, see pages:
_____
_____
_____

OBJECTIVE REVIEW NOTES

► Objective: Select the appropriate hardware and software tools to monitor trends in the network.

☐ Got it!   ☐ Review it!   ☐ Help!
   Date:_____   Date:_____   Date:_____

Notes:

_____
_____
_____
_____
_____

Fast Track cross-reference, see pages:

_____
_____

Other resources cross-reference, see pages:

_____
_____
_____

Troubleshooting

► Objective: Identify common errors associated with components required for communications.

☐ Got it!   ☐ Review it!   ☐ Help!
   Date:_____   Date:_____   Date:_____

Notes:

_____
_____
_____
_____
_____

Fast Track cross-reference, see pages:

_____
_____

Other resources cross-reference, see pages:

_____
_____
_____

OBJECTIVE REVIEW NOTES

► Objective: Diagnose and resolve common connectivity problems with cards, cables, and related hardware.

☐ **Got it!**
Date:_____

☐ **Review it!**
Date:_____

☐ **Help!**
Date:_____

Notes:

_____
_____
_____
_____
_____
_____

Fast Track cross-reference, see pages:

_____
_____

Other resources cross-reference, see pages:

_____
_____
_____
_____

► Objective: Resolve broadcast storms.

☐ **Got it!**
Date:_____

☐ **Review it!**
Date:_____

☐ **Help!**
Date:_____

Notes:

_____
_____
_____
_____
_____
_____

Fast Track cross-reference, see pages:

_____
_____

Other resources cross-reference, see pages:

_____
_____
_____

OBJECTIVE REVIEW NOTES

► Objective: Identify and resolve network performance problems.

☐ **Got it!**	☐ **Review it!**	☐ **Help!**
Date:	*Date:*	*Date:*

Notes:

_____
_____
_____
_____
_____
_____

Fast Track cross-reference, see pages:

_____

Other resources cross-reference, see pages:

_____
_____
_____
_____

OBJECTIVE REVIEW NOTES

Inside Exam 70-058

Part II of this book is designed to round out your exam preparation by providing you with chapters that do the following:

▶ "Fast Facts Review"is a digest of all "What is Important to Know" sections from all Part I chapters. Use this chapter to review just before you take the exam: It's all here, in an easily reviewable format.

▶ "Insider's Spin on Exam 70-058" grounds you in the particulars for preparing mentally for this examination and for Microsoft testing in general.

▶ "Sample Test Questions" provides a full length practice exam that tests you on the actual material covered in Part I. If you mastered the material there, you should be able to pass with flying colors here.

▶ "Hotlist of Exam-Critical Concepts" is your resource for cross-checking your tech terms. Although you're probably up to speed on most of this material already, double-check yourself anytime you run across an item you're not 100 percent certain about; it could make a difference at exam time.

▶ "Did You Know?" is the last-day-of-class bonus chapter: A brief touching-upon of peripheral information designed to help people using this technology to the point that they want to be certified in its mastery.

5   Fast Facts Review

6   Insider's Spin on Exam 70-058

7   Sample Questions

8   Hotlist of Exam-Critical Concepts

9   Did You Know?

OBJECTIVES

The exam is divided into four objective categories:

▶ **Standards and Terminology**

▶ **Planning**

▶ **Implementation**

▶ **Troubleshooting**

CHAPTER 5

Fast Facts Review

WHAT TO STUDY

This chapter is a review of the key topics discussed in the preceding four chapters. After you are certain that you understand the principles given in those chapters, study these key points on the day of the exam prior to taking it.

Standards and Terminology

Memorize the OSI model, the type of data each layer works with, hardware devices, and everything else listed in Table 5.1. (Use the mnemonic **All People Seem To Need Data Processing** to memorize the order of the layers.)

TABLE 5.1

OSI LAYERS

Layer	Purpose	Data Type	Hardware
Application	Interface to network services	Message	Gateway
Presentation	Translates between Application and all others; redirector; encryption; compression	Packet	Gateway
Session	Establishes rules for communication; synchronization	Packet	Gateway
Transport	Handles network transmission	Datagram, segment (and packet)	Gateway
Network	Addressing; traffic; switching	Datagram (and packet)	Router: Uses routing table; can determine best path; can be static or dynamic; can support multiple paths

Layer	Purpose	Data Type	Hardware
Data Link	Error checking; manages link control; communicates with card	Frame	Bridge: Uses MAC addresses; can connect different media and unlike segments
Physical	The connection, wire, cards, etc: what you can see and touch	Bits and signals	Repeater: No filtering or processing, just regeneration; can connect different media

Headers are added to the message as it travels down the layers and are stripped from the message as it travels up the layers. Brouters operate at both the Data Link and Network layer and function as both a bridge and a router.

Most protocols are **routable**, so it is easier to remember those that are not: **NetBEUI, DLC, and LAT** (a DEC protocol). Table 5.2 lists the IEEE 802 standards.

TABLE 5.2

THE IEEE 802 STANDARDS

802.1	Internetworking
802.2	**Logical Link Control**
802.3	**Carrier Sense with Multiple Access and Collision Detection (CSMA/CD)**
802.4	Token Bus LAN
802.5	Token Ring LAN
802.6	Metropolitan Area Network (MAN)
802.7	Broadband Technical Advisory Group
802.8	**Fiber Optic Tech Advisory Group**
802.9	Integrated Voice/Data Networks
802.10	Network Security
802.11	**Wireless Networks**
802.12	Demand Priority Access LAN, 100BaseVG AnyLAN

Fault tolerance can be provided by **stripe sets** with **parity** (RAID level 5) or **mirror sets** (RAID level 1). Both allow data to be recovered in the event of a system or hardware failure. Stripe sets with parity require a minimum of three physical disks, and the system and boot partitions can't be a part of the stripe set.

Disk striping without parity (RAID level 0) requires only two disks and **is not a fault-tolerant solution** since data can't be recovered in the event of a disk failure (no data redundancy). Its major benefit is that it offers the highest level of read and write performance of any of the available disk-management systems, allowing concurrent requests to be processed on all drives simultaneously.

Disk striping with parity always uses the smallest amount of free space on any drive, because the amount is then used on all other drives. Thus, if you have 100, 200, 300, and 400 MB free on each of four drives, only 100 MB would be used on each drive. Four times 100 MB means the stripe set would be 400 MB in size. Of that, one-fourth is used for storing parity information, so only 300 MB of data can be stored on the stripe set.

Disk mirroring can support only two hard drives and amounts to two drives running off the same controller. **Disk duplexing is the same as mirroring, except that it uses two disk controllers** instead of one (a hardware enhancement versus a software enhancement). **Mirror sets** are the only form of fault tolerance that can include system and boot partitions.

Planning

It is essential that you know the different **cable types** (as well as wireless) and **the benefits and restrictions of each**, as listed in Table 5.3.

TABLE 5.3

THE DIFFERENT CABLE TYPES

Cable	Cost	Installation	Capacity	Range	EMI
Thinnet	Less than STP and more than UTP	Easy	Typically 10 MBps	185 meters	Less sensitive than UTP
Thicknet	More than STP and less than fiber	Not as easy as Thinnet	Typically 10 MBps	500 meters	Less sensitive than UTP
Shielded Twisted Pair (STP)	More than UTP and less than Thicknet	Relatively easy	From 16 MBps to 500 MBps	100 meters	Less sensitive than UTP
Unshielded Twisted Pair (UTP)	Cheapest	Easy	10 MBps to 100 MBps	100 meters	Most sensitive of all
Fiber Optic	Most expensive	Hard	Typically 100 MBps	Kilo-meters	Least sensitive of all

Of particular importance in wiring are the 802.3 Ethernet types and the topology that they operate under. Know the maximum number of segments (and PCs per segment for each), as well as adapter type. See Table 5.4.

TABLE 5.4

THE 802.3 ETHERNET TYPES

Type	Connector	Terminated	Maximum Segments	Maximum PCs Per Segment	Maximum Network Length	Maximum Cable Length	Cable	Topology
10Base2	BNC	Yes	5	30	925 meters	185 meters	RG-58 Thinnet	Bus
10Base5	DIX/AUI	Yes	5	100	2500 meters	500 meters	Thicknet	Bus
10BaseT	RJ-45	No	N/A	1 per hub port—1, 024 on LAN	N/A	100 meters	UTP or STP of category 3, 4, or 5	Star

The category of the cable directly affects the speed: Cat 3 can go to 10 MBps, Cat 4 to 16 MBps, and Cat 5 to 100 MBps. With the bus topology, a single cable connects all the computers in a single line. With star, the computers are connected to a hub through cable segments. Not relevant to Ethernet is the ring topology, where all the computers are on a single wire that forms a loop.

Wireless media can be of several different types. The four most common, ranked in order of cost, are infrared, laser, narrow-band radio, and spread-spectrum radio.

Here are common IRQ settings for a computer:

0. System timer
1. Keyboard
2. Video card (EGA/VGA, and so on)
3. COM 2 or 4
4. COM 1 or 3
5. **Available**
6. Floppy disk
7. LPT 1
8. Real-time clock
9. **Available**
10. **Available**
11. **Available**
12. PS/2 mouse
13. Math coprocessor
14. Hard disk
15. **Available**

Switching is a vast improvement on routing that allows multiple paths to be used to deliver the data. **This decreases the amount of time necessary for delivery** and provides redundancy in paths. Three types of switching technologies are currently employed: circuit, message, and packet.

Circuit switching establishes a path that remains fixed for the duration of the connection. It's similar to telephone switching equipment. In the telephone world, switching equipment establishes a route between your telephone in the Midwest and a telephone in New York and maintains that connection for the duration of your call. The next time you call, the same path may or may not be used.

The advantages of circuit switching include the use of dedicated paths and a well-defined bandwidth. The disadvantages include the establishment of each connection (which can be time-consuming) and the inability of other traffic to share the dedicated media path. The latter can lead to inefficiently utilized bandwidth. Due to the need to have excess (or, rather, a surplus of) bandwidth, the technology tends to be expensive when compared to other options.

Message switching treats each message as an independent entity and isn't concerned with what came before or will come after. Each message carries its own address information and details of its destination. The information is used at each switch to transfer the message to the next switch in the route. Message switches are programmed with information concerning other switches in the network that can be used to forward messages to their destinations. They can also be programmed with information about which of the routes is the most efficient, and they can send different messages through the network to the same destination via different routes (and routers).

In message switching, the complete message is sent from one switch to the next, and the whole message is stored there before being forwarded. Because the switches hold what is coming in and wait until it is all there before sending anything out, they are often called store-and-forward networks. Common uses of such technology include email, calendaring, and groupware applications.

The advantages of message switching are that it can use relatively low-cost devices, data channels are shared among communicating devices, priorities can be assigned to manage traffic, and bandwidth is used rather efficiently. The disadvantage is that it is completely unacceptable for real-time applications.

When most administrators think of adding switches to their network, they think of packet switches. Here, messages are divided into smaller packets, each containing source and destination address information. They can be routed through the internetwork independently. Packet size is restricted to the point where the entire packet can remain in the memory of the switching devices, and there is no need to temporarily store the data anywhere. For this reason, packet switching routes the data through the network much more rapidly and efficiently than is possible with message switching.

There are many types of **packet switches**. The most common are **datagram** and **virtual circuit**. With datagram packet switching, each switch node decides which network segment should be used for the next step in the packet's route. This allows switches to bypass busy segments and take other steps to speed packets through the internetwork—making datagram packet switching ideally suited for LANs.

Virtual circuit packet switching establishes a formal connection between two devices and negotiates communication parameters, such as the maximum message size, communication window, network path, and so on, thus creating a virtual circuit that remains in effect until the devices stop communicating. When a virtual circuit is present on a temporary basis, you'll hear the buzzword switched virtual circuit (SVC). When the virtual circuit is present for an undetermined amount of time, the buzzword used is permanent virtual circuit (PVC).

The most popular implementation of packet switching is **ATM** (asynchronous transfer mode), which uses fixed-length **53-byte packets** (which ATM advocates call cells) and sends them across the internetwork. Because the size of 53 bytes is standard, the process of negotiating packet size with each connection is eliminated, thus allowing for an increase in transfer speed.

Regardless of the technology employed, **packet switching advantages** include the ability to optimize the use of bandwidth and enable many devices to route packets through the same network channels. At any time, a switch may be routing packets to several different destination devices, adjusting the routes as required to get the best efficiency possible. The only **disadvantage** is the initial cost of the equipment, which can be sizeable.

Implementation

There are several technologies and utilities to be familiar with in this section. Table 5.5 lists the technologies for packet switching and WAN.

TABLE 5.5

THE TECHNOLOGIES FOR PACKET SWITCHING AND **WAN**

Technology	Spelled-Out Name	Features
ATM	Asynchronous Transfer Mode	155 MBps to 622 MBps packet switching with all data being exactly 53-byte cells.
FDDI	Fiber Distributed Data Interface	100 MBps technology capable of connecting 62 miles (100 kilometers) per ring.
Frame relay	N/A	A point-to-point system across leased lines through the use of a bridge or router.
ISDN	Integrated Services Digital Network	A three-channel, dial-up, 128 Kbps technology that performs link management and signaling
RAS	Remote Access Service	Lets remote connections connect to a server. NT Server allows for 256 RAS connections.
SMDS	Switched Multimegabit Data Service	Offered by telephone companies. Uses ATM-like fixed-length cells and can reach speeds of 45 MBps.
SONET	Synchronous Optical Network	Can carry voice, data, and video at up to 1 GBps using multiplexing.
Switched 56	N/A	A nondedicated, circuit-switched version of a standard leased line.

Technology	Spelled-Out Name	Features
T1 and T3	N/A	A leased line from the phone company that uses multiplexers to obtain high speed or break a signal into channels. A T1 can operate at up to 1.544 MBps and can be divided into 24 voice channels. A T3 can operate at up to 44.736 MBps and be divided into 672 voice channels. A good way to remember the difference is that a T1 is 1/28th of a T3.
X.25	N/A	Connects at low-cost remote terminals to mainframe hosts through Public Data Networks (PDNs) and does error-checking (which slows it down).

The Remote Access Service can use TCP/IP, NWLink, or NetBEUI protocols for dial-in and dial-out connections. Of the three protocols, TCP/IP benefits from being routable, from being available on a number of different platforms, and from being *the* compatibility choice of the Internet. NWLink (which is IPX/SPX-compatible) is also routable, while NetBEUI is not.

Point-to-Point Protocol (**PPP**) is a **low-cost method** (in terms of administration) **of providing Internet access** to users while maintaining security. It allows any RAS client to run applications by using a number of technologies, including Remote Procedure Calls, Windows Socket APIs, and named pipes. RAS supports three modem protocols—RAS, PPP, and SLIP. SLIP requires little overhead but offers nothing in the way of error checking or security, and it's never the best choice unless you need connectivity with older Unix systems. PPP offers error checking and flow control, but requires slightly more overhead.

Here are the tools and utilities to be familiar with for this section:

- Performance Monitor
- Network Client Administrator
- Gateway Services for NetWare

The **Performance Monitor is NT's all-around tool for monitoring** a network by using statistical measurements called counters. It has the ability to collect data on both hardware and software components, called objects, and its primary purpose is to establish a baseline from which everything can be judged. It offers the ability to monitor such things as the demand for resources, bottlenecks in performance, the behavior of individual processes, and the performance of remote systems.

Every object has a number of counters. Some to be familiar with are those for the Paging File object—%Usage and %Usage Peak, which tell you if a paging file is reaching its maximum size.

To get numerical statistics, use the Report (columnar) **view.** To see how counters change over a period of time, use the log feature. To spot abnormalities that occur in data over a period of time, use the **Chart view.** Remember, **you** *must* **install the Network Monitor Agent in order to be able to see several network performance counters, and the SNMP service** *must* **be installed in order to gather TCP/IP statistics.**

To monitor a number of servers and be alerted if a counter exceeds a specified number, create one Performance Monitor alert for each server on your workstation. Enter your user name in the Net Name box in the Alert Options dialog box (under the Send Network Message tab), and you will be alerted when the alert conditions arise. Only one name can be placed here. The name can be that of a user or group, but can't be multiple users or groups.

If you are monitoring a number of performance counters and that **monitoring is slowing down** other operations on your workstation, the best remedy is to **increase the monitoring interval**.

In order to start an over-the-network installation of client operating systems (including Network Client 3.0 for MS-DOS, LAN Manager, or Windows for Workgroups), you need to create a Network Installation Startup Disk by using Network Client Administrator on the NT server. The disk contains the files needed to allow a client to connect to the network and access the installation files on the server. Once the startup disk is created, it can be used from the client machine to run the installation process.

At the workgroup level, the only security available is share-level security. At the domain level, clients (including Windows 95) support, but do not provide, user-level security. A Windows NT server or NetWare server is needed for user-level security authentication.

In order for clients to be able to access a NetWare server without using NetWare client software, you must install Gateway Service for NetWare on an NT server, create a group called NTGATEWAY on the NetWare server, include the user in the group, and map a drive that can be shared by the clients.

Troubleshooting

The NT system log contains information about services and drivers that fail to start. This file should always be examined with Event Viewer if a service fails to start. Event Viewer (located in the Administrative Tools program group) is a stand-alone utility used to examine the system log. It is not part of the Emergency Repair Process. When you're looking at a number of Stop errors in the system log via Event Viewer, the Stop error at the bottom of the list is generally the cause of all others since entries are written to the top of the file as they occur.

When a partition in a mirror set (RAID 1) or a stripe set with parity (RAID 5) fails, it becomes an orphan. **To fix a mirror set, you must first break it by choosing Fault Tolerance | Break Mirror**. This action exposes the remaining partition as a separate volume. The healthy partition is given the drive letter that was previously assigned to it in the set, and the orphaned partition is given the next logical drive letter, or one that you manually selected for it.

After the mirror has been reestablished as a primary partition, selecting additional free space and restarting the process of creating a mirror set can form a new relationship.

A stripe set with parity keeps a system running during the failure of one drive, but can't handle more than that. The **Regenerate command is used to reestablish a stripe set with parity after you replace the faulty disk.**

NT's Disk Administrator is the utility for all disk-related operations. If you don't have a current Emergency Repair Disk, Disk Administrator can restore the Registry key.

The three main parameters that specify how TCP/IP is configured are

- **The IP address (the computer's network address and host address)**

- **The subnet mask (specifies what portion of the IP address specifies the network address and what portion of the address specifies the host address)**

- **The default gateway (most commonly the address of the router)**

Using a DHCP server can greatly reduce TCP/IP configuration problems. Scopes are ranges of available addresses on a DHCP server. The most important part of the configuration is to make sure you don't have duplicate addresses in the different scopes.

Utilities to use in TCP/IP-related troubleshooting include the following:

- **ARP**. Displays the Address Resolution Protocol cache of MAC addresses.

- **IPCONFIG**. Displays the IP configuration information for the host. Should be used with the /ALL parameter to see DNS, WINS, DHCP, and NetBIOS information.

- **NBTSTAT**. Displays NetBIOS names. NetBIOS names are cached as they are resolved.

- **NETSTAT**. Displays all the TCP/IP protocol statistics.

- **NSLOOKUP**. Displays DNS server entry information.

- **PING**. Used with either IP addresses or host names (if there is a method to resolve them to IP addresses) to verify that you can get to another host.

- **ROUTE**. Displays the routing table and lets you add entries with ROUTE ADD or look at the table with ROUTE PRINT.

- **TRACERT**. An improvement over PING that traces the route being taken by the packet and displays the route hops.

Tools that can be used to troubleshoot the physical network include the following:

- **Digital Volt Meter. Troubleshoots cabling problems by checking voltage and resistance.**

- **Network Monitor. Can dissect packets and look for errors, collisions, and traffic to and from individual computers.**

- **Oscilloscope. An all-purpose tool for measuring signal voltage over time. It can be used to find shorts.**

- **Protocol Analyzer. Can be used to examine a packet and look for problems with the protocol itself (such as traffic, connections, errors, and so on).**

- **Time-Domain Reflectors. Send sound wave pulses through cable and look for breaks.**

When working with networking cabling problems, check the following:

- Make sure that connector pins are correct and crimped tightly. Look for bent or broken pins.

- Make sure that all the component cables in a segment are connected. A user who moves his client and removes the T-connector incorrectly can cause a broken segment.

- Look for electrical interference (power cords, fluorescent lights, electric motors, and so on).

- On coaxial Ethernet LANs, look for missing terminators or improper impedance ratings. With 10BASE-T, make sure the cable used has the correct number of twists to meet the data-grade specifications. Watch out for malfunctioning transceivers, concentrators, or T-connectors.

When working with network adapter card problems, check the following:

- **Make sure that the cable is properly connected to the card** and that you have the correct network adapter card driver.

- Make certain that the card is bound to the right transport protocol, and that both are compatible with your operating system.

- **Look for resource conflicts**, making certain that another device isn't attempting to use the same resources.

- If there is a conflict, run the network adapter card's diagnostic software.

- **Pull the card and reseat it, making certain that it fits properly in the slot.**

- Replace the card with one that you know works. If the connection works with a different card, you know the card is the problem.

Aside from these problems, it's always a good idea to apply common sense to troubleshooting. When looking at a problem, try to isolate it as much as possible and determine its scope. Obviously, if one network user out of 100 can't print to a printer, you don't replace the printer.

Although every problem is different, a common mindset should be applied to all of them. For example, if a user calls to report that he can't print to a particular printer, here is a sample methodology that you could apply:

1. Have you ever printed to that printer?

2. When what the last time you printed there (it could have been last year)?

3. What has changed since then?

4. Is anyone else experiencing the same problem?

5. Can you print from another application?

6. Can you print from another workstation?

7. Can you print to any printer?

At any point in this sequence, a red flag can pop up and trigger an immediate solution. Also, never overestimate the obvious—things such as power to the device, paper in the bin, and so on.

In the Insider's Spin, you get the author's word on exam details specific to 70-058, as well as information you possibly didn't know—but could definitely benefit from—about what's behind Microsoft's exam preparation methodology. This chapter is designed to deepen your understanding of the entire Microsoft exam process. Use it as an extra edge—inside info brought to you by someone who teaches this material for a living.

CHAPTER 6

Insider's Spin on Exam 70-058

At A Glance: Exam Information

Exam number	70-058
Minutes	75*
Questions	58*
Passing score	793*
Single-answer questions	Yes
Multiple-answer with correct number given	Yes
Multiple-answer without correct number given	Yes
Ranking order/solutions	No
Choices of A-D	Yes
Choices of A-E	Very few
Objective categories	4

Note: These exam criteria will no longer apply when this exam goes to an adaptive format.

Exam 70-058, Networking Essentials, is computer-administered and is intended to measure your ability to implement, administrate, and manage a network. There are 58 questions, and you have 75 minutes to answer them with a passing score of at least 793 (which roughly translates to passing with 46 correct answers).

The exam has three types of multiple-choice questions: single-answer (these questions have a radio button), multiple-answer with the correct number given, and a few multiple-answer without the correct number given. Most questions have four possible answers, but a few have five.

Although Microsoft no longer releases specific exam information, at one time it was noted that 85 percent of those who take a certification exam fail it. Therefore, logic indicates that only 15 out of every 100 people who think they know a product know it well enough to pass—a remarkably low number.

Quite often, administrators who *do* know a product very well and use it on a daily basis fail certification exams. Is it because they don't know the product as well as they think they do? Sometimes, but more often than not, it is because of other factors:

- They know the product from the real-world perspective, not Microsoft's perspective.

- They are basing their answers on the product as it currently exists, not on the product when it was first released.

- They are unaccustomed to so many questions in such a short time, or they are unaccustomed to the electronic test engine.

- They don't use all of the testing tools available to them.

The purpose of this chapter is to try to prepare you for the exam and help you overcome the four points just listed. If you've been taking exams on a daily basis, and you don't think you need this information, skim this chapter and go on. Odds are that you will still uncover some tips that can help you. On the other hand, if you haven't taken many electronic exams, or you've been having difficulty passing them by as wide a margin as you should, read this chapter carefully.

GET INTO MICROSOFT'S MIND-SET

When taking the exams, remember that Microsoft is the party responsible for the authoring of the exam. Microsoft employees do not actually write the exams themselves. Instead, experts in the field are hired on a contract basis to write questions for each exam. All questions must adhere to certain standards and be approved by Microsoft before they make it into the actual exam. What that translates to is that Microsoft will never have anything in an exam that reflects negatively on them. They will also use the exams for promotional marketing as much as possible.

Therefore, in order to successfully answer the questions and pass the exams, you must put yourself into the Microsoft mind-set and see the questions from their standpoint. Consider the following example:

1. Which network operating system is the easiest to administer in a small real estate office?

     A. NetWare 3.12

     B. SCO Unix

     C. Windows NT 4.0

     D. LAN Server

Although you could make a sincere argument for at least three of the answers, only one will be correct on a Microsoft exam. Don't try to read too much between the lines, and don't think that you can put a comment at the end of the exam arguing why another choice would be better. If you answer anything other than C, you might as well write this one off as a missed question.

UNDERSTAND THE EXAM'S TIMEFRAME

When you take an exam, find out when it was written. In almost all cases, an exam goes live within three months of the final release of the product it is based on. Prior to the exam's release, the exam goes through a beta process in which all the potential questions are written. It is then available for a short time (typically a week), during which scores on each question can be gathered. Questions that exam-takers consistently get right are weeded out as being too easy, and those that are too hard are also weeded out.

When you take something such as a major operating system and create an exam for it, you end up with a timeframe similar to the following:

1. The product goes into early beta.

2. A survey is done (mostly of beta testers) to find out which components of the product they spend the most time with and which they consider the most important. Their findings are used to generate the objectives and the weighting for each.

3. The product goes into final beta.

4. Contract writers are hired to write questions on the product using the findings from the survey.

5. The product goes live.

6. The exam is beta-tested for one to two weeks. The results of each question are evaluated, and the final question pool is chosen.

7. The service pack for the product is released.

8. The exam goes live.

9. Another service pack to fix problems from the first service pack and add additional functionality is released.

10. Yet another service pack comes out.

11. An option pack that incorporates service packs is released.

12. You take the exam.

Now suppose the product happens to be NT Server 4, and you see a question like this:

1. What is the maximum number of processors that NT Server 4.0 can handle?

   A. 2

   B. 4

   C. 8

   D. More than 8

In the real world, the answer is D. When NT 4.0 first came out, however, the answer was B. Since the original exam questions were written to the final beta, the answer then was B, and now is B. Microsoft has maintained that they will test only on core products, not add-ons. Service packs, option packs, and the like are considered something other than core product.

With this in mind, you must *always* answer every question as if you're addressing the product as it exists when you pull it from the box, and before you do anything with it—because that is exactly what the exam is written to. You must get into this mind-set and understand the timeframe in which the exam was written, or you will fail the exams consistently.

GET USED TO ANSWERING QUESTIONS QUICKLY

Every exam has a different number of questions, and most stick with the 90-minute timeframe (although Networking Essentials remains at 75). If you run out of time, every question you haven't answered is graded as wrong. Therefore, keep the following in mind:

- Always answer every question; never leave any unanswered. If you start running out of time, answer all the remaining questions with the same letter (C, D, and so on), and then go back and start reading them. Using the law of averages, if you do run out of time, you should get 25 percent of the remaining questions correct.

- Time yourself carefully. A clock runs at the top-right of each screen. Mark all the questions that require lots of reading, or that have exhibits, and come back to them after you've answered all of the shorter questions.

- Practice, practice, practice. Get accustomed to electronic questioning and answering questions in a short period of time. With as many exam simulators as there are available, you should run through one or two before plunking down $100 for the real thing. Some simulators aren't worth the code they're written in, and others are so close in style to the actual exam that they prepare you very well. If money is an issue, and it should be, look for demos and freebies on Web sites. http://www.MeasureUp.com is an excellent place to try some sample exams online.

When you have almost run out of time, spend as much time as you want to on the last question. You will never time out with a question in front of you. You will be timed out only when you click Next to go to the next question.

BECOME ACQUAINTED WITH ALL THE RESOURCES AVAILABLE TO YOU

An enormous amount of common sense is important here. You gain much of that common sense only as you get used to the testing procedure. Here's a typical sequence of events:

1. You study for an exam for a considerable period of time.

2. You call Sylvan Prometric (1-800-755-EXAM) and register for the exam.

3. You drive to the testing site, sit in your car, and cram on last-minute details.

4. You walk into the center, sign your name, show two forms of ID, and walk to a computer.

5. Someone enters your ID in the computer and leaves. You're left with the computer, two pieces of plain paper, and two #2 pencils.

6. You click the button on the screen to begin the exam, and the 75 minutes begins.

When you call Sylvan, be certain to ask how many questions are on the exam so that you will know before you go in. Sylvan is allowed to release very little information (for example, they can't tell you the passing score), but this is one of the few pieces of information they *can* pass along.

The exam begins the minute you click the button to start the exam. Prior to that time, your 75 minutes haven't started. Once you walk into the testing center and sit down, you're free to do whatever you want to (within reason). Why not dump everything from your brain (including those last-minute facts you studied in the parking lot) onto those two sheets of paper before you start the exam? The two sheets give you four sides—more than enough to scribble down everything you remember and refer to during the 75 minutes.

After you click Start, the first question appears. A number of different types of questions are asked; Figure 6.1 shows but one. Since Microsoft doesn't readily make available screen shots of the exams (for obvious reasons), all the figures in this chapter are from a third-party emulator that closely resembles the real thing.

Look at the question briefly, but more importantly, look at the information on the screen. First, you have the ability to mark a question, so that at the end of the exam you can review all the questions you thought were too difficult and jump back to them. Never mark a question and go to the next one without choosing an answer. Even if you don't read the question at all, and you're saving it for later, mark it and answer C. That way, if you run out of time, you have a chance of getting it right.

In the right corner, you see the number of the question you are on. In the real exam, you also see the time remaining. Beneath the question are the possible answers. The radio buttons to the left of each indicate that there is only one answer.

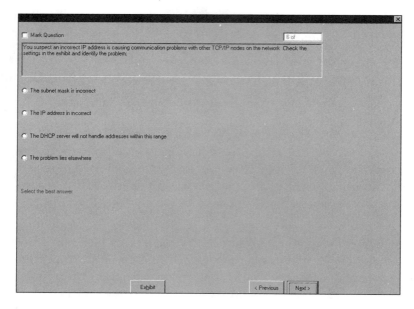

FIGURE 6.1
A sample test question.

Although this isn't always true, many times when there are four possibilities, one will be so far off the mark as to not even be a possibility, and another will be too much of a gimme to be true, so you are left with two possibilities that you must choose between. For example:

1. In NT Server 4.0, to view the Application log, what tool must you use?

   A. Application Viewer

   B. Event Viewer

   C. Event Observer

   D. Performance Monitor

In this case, choice A is the gimme, because it lists a nonexistent tool that fits the question too perfectly. Choice D is the blow-off answer—so far away from what's possible as to not be a possibility. That leaves choices B and C.

Even if you knew nothing about NT Server, a clue that B and C are legitimate possibilities is the closeness in the wording. Any time you see two answers worded so similarly, assume that they are the ones to focus on.

The buttons at the bottom of the screen let you move to the next question or to a previous question. The latter is important, because if you ever come across a question in which the wording provides the answer to a question you saw before, always use the Previous button to go back and change or check your answer. Never walk away from a sure thing.

If there is an exhibit associated with the question, the command button for it will be displayed as well. The problem with exhibits is that they appear on top of the question, or they can be tiled in such a way that you can't see either. Whenever you have an exhibit, read the question carefully, open the exhibit, memorize what is there (or scribble information about it on your sheet of paper), close the exhibit, and answer the question.

Figure 6.2 shows an example of a question that has more than one correct answer, as evidenced by the check boxes appearing to the left of the choices instead of radio buttons.

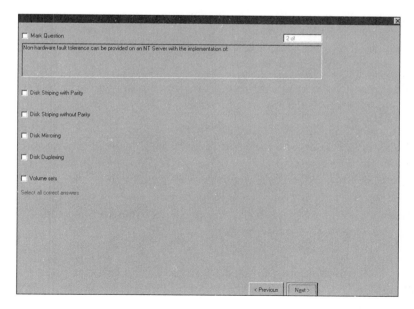

FIGURE 6.2
Another sample test question.

There are two types of these questions—one where you are told how many answers are correct (choose two, choose three, and so on), and another where you are not. In Figure 6.2, you are told to choose all the correct answers, and you don't know if that is two, three, or four. The only thing you do know is that it isn't one or five. Microsoft doesn't use check boxes if radio buttons will work, and you will never see an all-of-the-above type of question.

The vast majority of multiple-answer questions offer four possibilities, meaning that you must choose two or three—but five possibilities are not uncommon (as shown in Figure 6.2). With these kinds of questions, read the question as carefully as possible, and begin eliminating choices. For example, the question in Figure 6.2 specifically says *non-hardware,* and one of the choices is duplexing. Duplexing requires a hardware enhancement over mirroring, so choice D is incorrect. You are left with four possibilities, and you must rely on your knowledge to choose the right ones.

The biggest problem with multiple answers is that there is no such thing as partial credit. If you are supposed to choose four items, and you choose only three, the question still counts as being wrong. If you choose two—one right answer and one wrong answer—you miss the whole question. Spend much more time with multiple-answer questions than single-answer questions, and always come back after the exam, if time allows, and reread them carefully.

After you complete the exam, if there is time remaining, you come to an item-review section, similar to the one shown in Figure 6.3.

Here you can see the questions that you marked and jump back to them. If you've already chosen an answer, it remains chosen until you choose something else (the question also remains marked until you unmark it). The command buttons at the bottom of the question include an Item Review choice to let you jump back to the item review screen without going through additional questions. "Incomplete" questions are marked in the item review with a red letter "I."

Use the ability to mark and jump as much as you possibly can. All lengthy questions should be marked and returned to in this manner. Also note all answers that are incomplete. You can ill afford to not answer any question, so be certain to go back and fill them in before choosing to finish the exam (or running out of time).

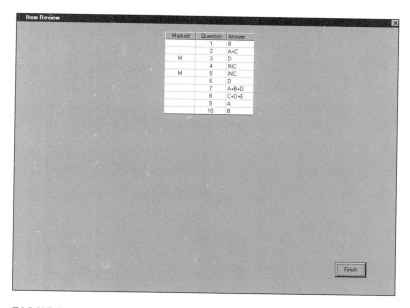

FIGURE 6.3
The item review at the completion of the exam.

After you click Finish, the grading is done, and the Examination Score Report appears. The one shown in Figure 6.4 is a bit misleading. Typically, the bar graphs appear and a message denotes passing or failing only. The Section Analysis doesn't appear on-screen, only on the printed documentation that you walk out of the testing center with. The pass/fail score is based on the exam beta and statistics gathered from the performance of those who took it.

If you fail an exam, and everyone will occasionally, *never* be lulled into a false sense of confidence by the Section Analysis. If it says you scored 100% in a particular section, you should still study that section before retaking the exam. Too many test-takers study only the sections they did poorly on. That 100% in Monitoring and Optimization could be the result of the first question pool containing only one question on that topic, and you had a 25 percent chance of guessing correctly. What happens next time when there are three questions in the random pool from that objective category, and you don't know the answers? You're handicapping yourself right off the bat.

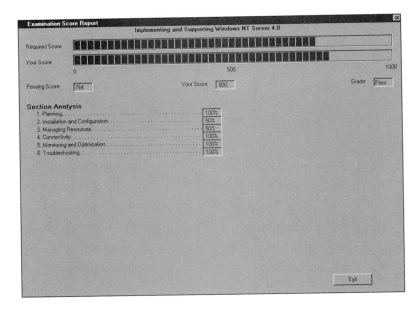

FIGURE 6.4
The Examination Score Report.

A good rule of thumb if you do fail an exam is to rush back to your car and write down all the questions you can remember. Have your study materials in the car with you and look up the answers then and there. If you wait until later, you'll forget many of them.

The new policy from Microsoft allows you to retake an exam you fail once without any waiting period (other than registering for it and so on). If you fail it again, however, you must wait 14 days before you can take it a third time (and 14 days from that point for the fourth try, and so on). This is to prevent people from memorizing the exam. Do your best to never fall into this category. If you fail an exam once, start all over again and study anew before trying it the second time. Make the second attempt within a week of the first, however, so that the topics are fresh in your mind.

WHERE THE QUESTIONS COME FROM

Knowing where the questions come from can be as instrumental as knowing how to prepare for the exam. The more you know about it, the better your odds of passing. Earlier, I discussed the time frame used to create the exam, and I mentioned that contract writers are hired for the exam. The contract writers are given a sizable document detailing how questions must be written. If you really want to pursue the topic with fervor, contact Microsoft and inquire about a contract writing position. Here are a few tidbits that can be gleaned from multiple-choice authoring:

+ No question should have an All of the Above answer. Such a question is not a fair representation of a valid multiple-choice question.

+ For the same reason, there should never be a None of the Above answer.

+ Scenarios should be used when they will increase the value of the question.

+ Subjective words such as best and most should be avoided.

+ Although there can be only one correct answer for the question, all other possibilities should appear plausible and avoid all rationale or explanations.

+ Single answers must be mutually exclusive (no A and C, B and C, and so on).

+ Negative words such as not and cannot should be avoided.

DIFFERENT FLAVORS OF QUESTIONS

At one time, all questions were either single-answer or multiple-answer. There is a push today to go more toward *ranking* questions and performance-based questions. Older exams still have only the first two types of questions, while newer ones offer the latter.

Ranking questions provide you with a scenario, a list of required objectives, a list of optional objectives, and a proposed solution. You have to rank how well the solution meets the objectives. Here's a rudimentary example:

1. Evan is a teenager who just got his driver's license. He wants to buy a fast car and ask Betty Lou to the movies on Friday.

   Required objectives: Buy a fast car.
                                          Ask Betty Lou to the movies.

   Optional objectives: Earn money for the movies.
                                          Earn money for a car.

   Solution: Take a part-time job at the Kwik-E-Mart and buy a classic '67 Cougar.

   Rank the solution in terms of the objectives:

   A. The solution meets both the required and the optional objectives.

   B. The solution meets both of the required objectives and only the first optional objective.

   C. The solution meets both of the required objectives and only the second optional objective.

   D. The solution does not meet the required objectives.

In this simple example, the answer is D. The solution doesn't include asking Betty Lou to the movies, so it doesn't meet the required objectives. With ranking questions, it is often the case that the required objectives are met in all but the last answer, so read the question backward, if you will, and see if the required objectives are being met. If they aren't, you can answer the question quickly without reading any further and go on to the next one.

Performance-based questions have been incorporated in electronic testing for a long time—just not with Microsoft testing. If I really wanted to see how well you knew a product before hiring you, the best way to do so would be to turn you loose with the product and tell you to do something. If you can, I'll hire you. If you can't, I won't.

Translating that scenario to the testing center becomes difficult. First and foremost, you can't be allowed unrestricted access to the product within the confines of something (a shell) that grades your actions. Second, the stability of the operations on most testing centers' antiquated machines is questionable at best. Last, the amount of time allotted can't exceed a reasonable amount, or you will become exhausted, and the testing center won't be able to move as many people through each day.

The solution to many of these problems is to keep the number of performance-based questions to a minimum and to have you work with an emulator of some type. The emulator can appear on-screen when you click the button and display something that looks like what the configuration information in the real product would be, without the time and overhead involved in bringing up the real product.

How do you prepare for performance-based questions? Know your product—plain and simple. If you focus on the administrative side of things—how to add new users, sites, servers, directories, and so on, you will have no difficulties. If you're good at guessing, but you really don't know the product, these questions will ferret that out. On the other hand, if you know your product extremely well, but you just aren't good at multiple-choice guessing, you'll find these questions a godsend.

Regardless of your familiarity with the product (or lack thereof), be very careful with the performance-based questions. Although the emulator can load much quicker than the actual product in question, it is still very time-consuming, and the amount of time required to answer each question is far from minute. These questions take *a lot* of time, so you need to budget for them accordingly.

IN THE FUTURE

The study of test delivery and grading is known as psychometrics, and a good many people are employed in this profession. Microsoft uses many of these people to help with the design and implementation of their exams. If you have any experience with other certifications, such as Novell's, it should come as no surprise that the next big push will be toward *adaptive* testing.

Under adaptive testing, the amount of time for each exam can be reduced from 90 minutes to somewhere near 30, and the number of questions can drop from 50 or 70 down to 15 or so. This benefits you greatly and also allows more students to be tested each day at training centers.

The premise behind adaptive testing is fairly simple: The first question you get is totally at random and pulled from a pool. After that first question, every subsequent question is related to how well you answered the preceding question.

For example, suppose I want to give you a general exam on astronomy. The first question asks you how many planets are in our solar system. You answer correctly (nine). I now ask you to name the third planet from the sun, and again you answer correctly (Earth). I can now assume that you know your planets very well, so the next question will be about quasars. We'll do this for 15 questions, and if you answer them all correctly, I'll assume that you really know astronomy and pass you.

If, on the other hand, you answered Mars to the second question, the next question would be about planets again—giving you a chance to redeem yourself. If you missed that one, I would probably ask you an extremely difficult question about planets to see if you can get it right. If you can't, you don't know planets, so you don't know astronomy, and you'll fail. In some versions of adaptive testing, you bomb out right then, because there is no chance of redemption. On others, you are given bogus questions for the remainder of the exam to make you feel like you're getting your money's worth, even though you will fail anyway.

Again, it differs per style and vendor, but with most adaptive tests, if you answer the 15 questions and haven't passed, but are very close to doing so, you can be asked additional questions. The additional questions give you the opportunity to redeem yourself and achieve a passing score.

The key to adaptive testing, besides each question's relationship to the one preceding it, is that every question has a point value. The first questions presented are of medium value. If you miss a question on a topic, the next one asked will be more difficult, and of a higher point value, to allow a chance for redemption. If you answer the first question correctly, the next one will be of lesser value and lesser difficulty.

There is no item review in adaptive testing, and there is no going back to the preceding questions. Once you answer a question, you are done with it, and you can draw a fair conclusion as to how you did by whether or not the next question is on a similar topic.

Performance-based testing is in its infancy at Microsoft, but it should be rolled out within the year. Again, the best preparation is to know your topic and to spend time with each question, making certain that you fully understand what is being asked before you answer. With performance-based testing, you are given a task to perform in an emulator of the product you are testing on. Your performance is graded to see if you accomplished the task within the time and manner in which an administrator should.

This is an exam preparation book. It's the belief of the author and publisher that it's difficult to get too much practice with sample exam questions. There are other study materials available—books and software—that enable you to practice extensively, and we recommend that you give strong consideration to using these in some form.*

What follows in this chapter is a practice test designed to reflect the questions you'd likely be challenged with on an actual Microsoft exam. These questions tie in directly to the material covered in this book. Take note that when this exam goes to an adaptive format, the number of questions, passing score, and minutes necessary to take this exam will vary.

*Please see the end matter of this book for more information on New Riders TestPrep books and New Riders Top Score exam preparation software, among other New Riders certification study resources.

CHAPTER 7

Sample Test Questions

QUESTIONS

This sample test has 58 questions, just like the actual exam, and covers each of the four objective categories. Please note: When this exam goes to an adaptive format, the number of questions, passing score, and minutes given to take the exam will vary.

1. *Which cable type supports the greatest cable length?*
   A. Unshielded twisted pair
   B. Shielded twisted pair
   C. Large coaxial cable
   D. Thin coaxial cable

2. *What two are advantages of UTP cable?*
   A. Low cost
   B. Easy installation
   C. High resistance to EMI due to twists in the cable
   D. Cables up to 500 meters

3. *You can use _____ to look for breaks in network cables by measuring cable voltage.*
   A. protocol analyzer
   B. DVM
   C. time-domain reflectometer
   D. MSDL

4. *Most network problems occur at the OSI _____ layer.*
   A. physical
   B. data link
   C. network
   D. session

5. *Which is not true of Ethernet boards?*
   A. Ethernet boards usually have DIX connectors.
   B. Ethernet boards can have thick (DIX), thin (BNC), or twisted pair (RJ-45) connectors.
   C. Ethernet boards have internal transceivers for Thinnet.
   D. Ethernet boards have a timeout setting.

6. *Which level of cable is correct for 10BASE-T?*
   A. Level I
   B. Level II
   C. Level III
   D. Level IV

7. *What are three advantages of coaxial cable?*
   A. Low cost
   B. Easy installation
   C. Good resistance to EMI
   D. Easy to reconfigure

8. *What are two benefits of shielding a cable?*
   A. Reduction in signal attenuation
   B. Reduction in EMI radiation
   C. Reduction in sensitivity to outside interference
   D. Easier cabling to splice center

9. *Rules that govern computer communications are called*
   _____.
   A. protocols
   B. layers
   C. services
   D. topologies

10. *Which two entities can share services on a network (select the two best answers)?*
    A. Servers
    B. Clients
    C. Peers
    D. Requesters

11. *What are three types of antennas?*
    A. Beam
    B. Duplex
    C. Dipole
    D. Random-length wire

12. *As frequency increases, radio transmission becomes increasingly*
    _____.

    A. attenuated
    B. rapid
    C. line-of-sight
    D. sensitive to electromagnetic interference

13. *Which of the following Ethernet frame types is designated as raw Ethernet?*

    A. ETHERNET_802.2
    B. ETHERNET_802.3
    C. ETHERNET_SNAP
    D. ETHERNET_II

14. *Which of the following is not an advantage of using 10BASE-T for cabling a network?*

    A. It is easier and more reliable to manage.
    B. Centralized hubs make it easier to detect bad cable segments.
    C. Beaconing helps isolate cable breaks.
    D. It is relatively inexpensive to use.

15. *A sudden, unexpected flood of broadcast messages on the network is known as* _____.

    A. net frenzy
    B. a tornado
    C. a broadcast storm
    D. an electric shower

16. *Possible causes of increased traffic include which two of the following?*

    A. A network computer game
    B. Power fluctuations
    C. A disorderly workstation shutdown
    D. A new workstation

17. *What is the most common cause of physical-layer problems (select the best answer)?*

    A. User error
    B. Aborted server calls
    C. Workstation GPFs
    D. Cabling

18. *What can send sound waves along a cable, looking for imperfections?*

    A. Time Domain Reflectometers
    B. Digital Volt Meters
    C. Protocol Analyzers
    D. TechNet

19. *Which two of the following are functions of internetwork connectivity devices?*

    A. Connecting remote networks
    B. Allowing networks with differing protocols to communicate
    C. Attaching devices to media
    D. Extending the range of network segments

20. *Which three of the following are advantages of active hubs?*

    A. They can regenerate network signals.
    B. LAN ranges can be extended.
    C. They are inexpensive.
    D. They function as repeaters.

21. *Which two of the following statements are true?*

    A. Coax Ethernet is a physical bus and a logical bus.
    B. 10BASE-T Ethernet is a physical bus and a logical bus.
    C. Coax Ethernet is a physical star and a logical bus.
    D. 10BASE-T Ethernet is a physical star and a logical bus.

22. *Which statement is true?*

    A. A physical star can't be a logical ring.
    B. Logical topologies are determined by the cabling system.
    C. A physical bus network may be a logical ring.
    D. Contention can be used as an access control medium on a physical ring.

23. *What are two advantages of bus topologies?*

    A. Long cable runs are possible without signal regeneration.
    B. They often require the least amount of cable.
    C. They are based on proven technology.
    D. They are easy to troubleshoot.

24. *Which three of the following are possible functions of the application layer?*

   A. Network printing service
   B. End-user applications
   C. Client access to network services
   D. Service advertisement

25. *Dialog control is a function of which OSI Reference Model layer?*

   A. Network
   B. Transport
   C. Session
   D. Presentation

26. *All signals transmitted between computers consist of some form of* _____.

   A. infrared light
   B. radio frequency
   C. microwave signal
   D. electromagnetic waveform

27. *Data transmission rates are often stated in terms of* _____.

   A. bits per second
   B. cycles per second
   C. attenuation
   D. resistance

28. *A network printer must traditionally stay within what limit from a network PC to function properly?*

   A. 5 feet
   B. 50 feet
   C. 100 feet
   D. Unlimited

29. *A printer attached directly to a PC must generally stay within what limit from the PC to function properly?*

   A. 5 feet
   B. 50 feet
   C. 100 feet
   D. Unlimited

30. *Protocol analyzers can identify which three of the following?*
   A. Malfunctioning network components
   B. Network cable voltage
   C. Bottlenecks
   D. Protocol problems

31. *Which two of the following statements about network analyzers are true?*
   A. They work primarily at the Physical layer.
   B. They are also known as protocol analyzers.
   C. They work at a number of upper OSI model layers.
   D. They analyze and display problems associated with cabling.

32. *Which connectivity device functions at the data link layer?*
   A. Repeater
   B. Router
   C. Hub
   D. Bridge

33. *Which two networks can use passive hubs?*
   A. Ethernet
   B. ARCnet
   C. Token Ring
   D. RAID-enabled

34. *The OSI model organizes communication protocols into how many layers?*
   A. 4
   B. 7
   C. 17
   D. 56

35. *Message data for any layer consists of which two of the following?*
   A. Datagram
   B. A protocol
   C. A header
   D. The data of the next-higher layer

36. *Which protocol layer lets multiple devices share the transmission medium?*

    A. Physical

    B. MAC

    C. LLC

    D. Network

37. *Which of the following is not an option for leased-line service?*

    A. T1

    B. X.14

    C. Frame relay

    D. ATM

38. *DIN connectors are primarily used for _____.*

    A. connecting UTP cables

    B. cabling Macintosh computers to AppleTalk networks

    C. connecting devices with Thick Ethernet

    D. identifying local loops beyond the demarc

39. *What are two wireless technologies that are sensitive to radio-frequency interference?*

    A. Microwave

    B. Spread-spectrum

    C. Infrared

    D. High-power single-frequency

40. *FDDI stands for _____.*

    A. Fiber-based Data Distribution Interface

    B. Fiber Distributed Data Interface

    C. Fiber-optic Data Distributed Interface

    D. Fiber Data Distribution Interface

41. *Which two features can add intelligence to a hub?*

    A. Signal regeneration

    B. Network management protocols

    C. Multiport repeaters

    D. Switching circuitry

42. *Which two statements are true of repeaters?*
   A. Repeaters amplify signals.
   B. Repeaters extend network distances.
   C. Repeaters regenerate signals.
   D. Repeaters can be used to extend a network's range indefinitely.

43. *Which two protocols are designed to provide reliable delivery?*
   A. IPX
   B. TCP
   C. UDP
   D. RAS

44. *Which protocol lets clients identify available NetWare servers?*
   A. IPX
   B. NLSP
   C. SAP
   D. RIP

45. *Which three protocols translate logical device names to device addresses?*
   A. DNS
   B. NBP
   C. SAP
   D. X.500

46. *An analysis of normal traffic patterns can help determine whether more _____ should be added to the network.*
   A. servers
   B. protocols
   C. layers
   D. utilities

47. *The purpose of fault management is to _____.*
   A. record and report the use of network resources
   B. detect and isolate network problems
   C. monitor, analyze, and control network data production
   D. monitor and control access to network resources

48. *Which two connectors are commonly used with coaxial cable?*
    A. DB-25
    B. N
    C. ST
    D. BNC

49. *Which two wireless technologies are good choices for connecting two buildings on opposite sides of a highway?*
    A. Satellite microwave
    B. High-power single-frequency
    C. Terrestrial microwave
    D. Broadcast infrared

50. *Which two statements are true of infrared systems?*
    A. Point-to-point infrared is not suitable for mobile stations.
    B. Infrared has a frequency range between 100 Ghz and 1,000 Thz.
    C. Due to reflection, neither point-to-point nor broadcast systems need be precisely aligned.
    D. Common interference can be caused by consumer products, such as garage door openers.

51. *What is one advantage that FDDI has over token ring?*
    A. Fiber-optic cable is difficult to wiretap.
    B. FDDI can isolate cable breaks.
    C. FDDI provides fair and timely access to the network.
    D. FDDI has built-in ring management.

52. *Which three Ethernet options require that each end of the bus be terminated?*
    A. 10BASE2
    B. 10BASE5
    C. 10BASE-T
    D. Thinnet

53. *The best way to reduce the effects of extra traffic caused by a network backup is to _____.*
    A. attach the tape drive directly to one of the servers
    B. back up each server to a nearby server
    C. place the computer attached to a tape drive on an isolated segment
    D. back up the servers in ascending order of the size of the backup

54. *Which network layer is concerned with data encryption?*
    A. Network
    B. Transport
    C. Session
    D. Presentation

55. *Which switching method makes the most efficient use of network bandwidth?*
    A. Message
    B. Circuit
    C. Packet
    D. Thread

56. *Which three statements are true?*
    A. Attenuation of radio waves is less with high-power signals.
    B. High-frequency radio LANs can penetrate office walls.
    C. Radio frequency LANs have high bandwidth.
    D. Spread-spectrum technology reduces sensitivity to EMI.

57. *Which statement is true?*
    A. Telephone wiring can be reliably used for most UTP networks.
    B. Thin coaxial networks are easy to install and reconfigure.
    C. Fiber-optic cable supports cable runs of tens of kilometers.
    D. STP cable is insensitive to EMI.

58. *Which three statements about bridges are true?*
    A. Bridges amplify and regenerate signals.
    B. Bridges can connect logically separate networks.
    C. Bridges use device address tables to route messages.
    D. Bridges divide networks into smaller segments.

ANSWERS

1. **C** Of the choices presented, large coaxial cable supports the greatest cable run length.

2. **A - B** UTP cable offers two distinct advantages: low cost of implementation, and ease of implementation.

3. **B** A Digital Volt Meter can be used to look for breaks in network cables by measuring cable voltage.

4. **A** Most network problems occur at the physical layer of the OSI model.

5. **D** Ethernet boards do not have a timeout setting.

6. **C** 10BASE-T uses Level III cabling when properly installed.

7. **A - B - C** Three advantages of coaxial cable are its low cost, easy installation, and resistance to EMI.

8. **B, C** Shielding a cable offers a reduction in EMI radiation and a reduction in sensitivity to outside interference.

9. **A** Rules that govern computer communications are called protocols.

10. **A - D** Two entities that can share services on a network are servers and requesters.

11. **A - C - D** Three types of antenna are beam, dipole, and random-length wire.

12. **C** As frequency increases, radio transmission becomes more line-of-sight oriented.

13. **B** ETHERNET_802.3 is designated as raw Ethernet.

14. **C** Beaconing to isolate cable breaks is not an advantage of using 10BASE-T for cabling a network.

15. **C** A sudden, unexpected flood of broadcast messages on the network is known as a broadcast storm.

16. **A - D**   Causes of increased traffic include networked computer games and new workstations.

17. **D**   The most common cause of physical-layer problems is cabling.

18. **A**   Time Domain Reflectometers can send sound waves along a cable, looking for imperfections.

19. **A - B**   Two functions of internetwork connectivity devices are connecting remote networks and allowing networks with differing protocols to communicate.

20. **A - C - D**   Three advantages of active hubs are that they can regenerate network signals, they are inexpensive, and they function as repeaters.

21. **A - D**   Coax Ethernet is a physical bus and a logical bus, and 10BASE-T Ethernet is a physical star and a logical bus.

22. **A**   A physical star can't be a logical ring.

23. **B - C**   Two advantages of bus topologies are that they often require the least amount of cable, and they are based on proven technology.

24. **A - C - D**   Three possible functions of the application layer are network printing service, client access to network services, and service advertisement.

25. **C**   Dialog control is a function of the Session layer in the OSI Reference Model.

26. **D**   All signals transmitted between computers consist of some form of electromagnetic waveform.

27. **A**   Data transmission rates are often stated in terms of bits per second.

28. **D**   A network printer is not limited to distance from a network PC to function properly, although it should be limited to the physical topology.

29. **B**   A printer attached directly to a PC must stay within 50 feet of the PC to function properly.

30. **A - C - D**   Protocol analyzers can identify malfunctioning network components, bottlenecks, and protocol problems.

31. **B - C**   Network analyzers are also known as protocol analyzers, and they work at a number of upper OSI model layers.

32. **D**   Bridges function at the data link layer.

33. **B - C**   ARCnet and Token Ring networks can use passive hubs.

34. **B**   The OSI model organizes communication protocols into seven layers.

35. **C - D**   Message data for any layer consists of a header and the data of the next-higher layer.

36. **B**   The MAC lets multiple devices share the transmission medium.

37. **B**   X.14 is not an option for leased-line service.

38. **B**   DIN connectors are primarily used for cabling Macintosh computers to AppleTalk networks.

39. **B - C**   Two wireless technologies that are sensitive to radio-frequency interference are spread-spectrum and infrared.

40. **B**   FDDI stands for Fiber Distributed Data Interface.

41. **B - D**   Two features that can add intelligence to a hub are network management protocols and switching circuitry.

42. **A - B**   Repeaters amplify signals and can extend network distances.

43. **B - C**   TCP and UDP are protocols designed to provide reliable delivery.

44. **C**   SAP lets clients identify available NetWare servers.

45. **A - B - D**   DNS, NBP, and X.500 are all protocols that can translate logical device names to device addresses.

46. **A**   An analysis of normal traffic patterns can help determine whether more servers should be added to the network.

47. **B**   The purpose of fault management is to detect and isolate network problems.

48. **B - D**   N-type and BNC are two connectors that are commonly used with coaxial cable.

49. **B - C**   Two wireless technologies that are good for connecting two buildings on opposite sides of a highway are high-power single-frequency and terrestrial microwave.

50. **A - B**   Point-to-point infrared is not suitable for mobile stations, and infrared has a frequency range between 100 Ghz and 1,000 Thz.

51. **A**   Fiber-optic cable is difficult to wiretap, and that provides an advantage over token ring.

52. **A - B - D**   10BASE2, 10BASE5, and Thinnet Ethernet require that each end of the bus be terminated.

53. **C**   The best way to reduce the effects of extra traffic caused by a network backup is to place the computer attached to a tape drive on an isolated segment.

54. **D**   The Presentation layer of the OSI model is concerned with data encryption.

55. **C**   Packet switching makes the most efficient use of network bandwidth.

56. **A - C - D**   Attenuation of radio waves is less with high-power signals, radio frequency LANs have high bandwidth, and spread-spectrum technology reduces sensitivity to EMI.

57. **C**   Fiber-optic cable supports cable runs of tens of kilometers.

58. **A - C - D**   Bridges amplify and regenerate signals, use device address tables to route messages, and divide networks into smaller segments.

If you feel the need to practice more exam questions, take a look at New Riders' MCSE TestPrep series of certification preparation books, featuring hundreds of review questions and concise explanations of why answer choices are correct or incorrect. These books are specifically designed for exam candidates who want to drill themselves extensively on exam questions.

The breadth and depth of your technical vocabulary is a significant measure of your knowledge as applied to the exam you're about to be tested on. The Hotlist of exam-critical concepts is something you should access every time you run across a term or a work you're not sure about. Double-check your knowledge by reviewing this section from time to time; do you have a slightly different definition for a term? Why? The answer can deepen your understanding of the technology.

Do you need to add your own definitions or new terms? It's more than likely, because no two exam candidates will find the same list of terms equally useful. That's why there's room to add your own terms and concepts at the end of this section.

CHAPTER 8

Hotlist of Exam-Critical Concepts

Term	*Definition*
ACK	Acknowledgment. A response from a receiving computer to a sending computer to indicate successful receipt of information. TCP requires that packets be acknowledged before it considers the transmission safe.
Active open	An action taken by a client to initiate a TCP connection with a server.
Address classes	A grouping of IP addresses with each class, defining the maximum number of networks and hosts available. The first octet of the address determines the class.
Address mask	A 32-bit binary number used to select bits from an IP address for subnet masking.
Address Resolution	A translation of an IP address to a Protocol (ARP) corresponding physical address.
Analog	A form of electronic communication using a continuous electromagnetic wave, such as television or radio. Any continuous wave form as opposed to digital on/off transmissions.
ANSI	American National Standards Institute. The membership organization responsible for defining U.S. standards in the information technology industry.
API	Application Programming Interface. A language and message format that lets a programmer use functions in another program or in the hardware.
ARP	Address Resolution Protocol. A protocol in the TCP/IP suite used to bind an IP address to a physical hardware (MAC) address.
ARPA	Advanced Research Projects Agency. A government agency that originally funded research on the ARPANET (which became DARPA in the mid-1970s).

Term	*Definition*
ARPANET	The first network of computers funded by the U.S. Department of Defense Advanced Projects Agency. An experimental communications network funded by the government that eventually developed into the Internet.
ASCII	American Standard Code for Information Interchange. Data that is limited to letters, numbers, and punctuation.
ATM	Asynchronous Transfer Mode. Broadband technology that increases transfer speeds.
Backbone	Generally very high-speed T3 telephone lines that connect remote ends of networks to one another. Only service providers are connected to the Internet in this way.
Baseband	A network technology that requires all nodes attached to the network to participate in every transmission. Ethernet is an example of a baseband technology.
BOOTP	Bootstrap protocol. A protocol used to configure systems with an IP address, a subnet mask, and a default gateway across internetworks.
Bps	Bits per second. A measurement that expresses the speed at which data is transferred between computers.
Bridge	A device that connects one physical section of a network to another, often providing isolation.
Broadband	A network technology that multiplexes multiple network carriers into a single cable.
Broadcast	A packet destined for all hosts on the network.

Term	*Definition*
Brouter	A computer device that works as both a bridge and a router. Some network traffic may be bridged, while other traffic is routed.
Buffer	A storage area used to hold input or output data.
Checksumming	A service performed by UDP that checks to see if packets were changed during transmission.
Connectionless service	A delivery service that treats each packet as a separate entity. Often results in lost packets or packets delivered out of sequence.
CRC	Cyclic Redundancy Check. A computation about a frame of which the result is a small integer. The value is appended to the end of the frame and recalculated when the frame is received. If the results differ from the appended value, the frame has presumably been corrupted and is therefore discarded. It is used to detect errors in transmission.
CSMA	Carrier Sense Multiple Access. A simple media access control protocol that allows multiple stations to contend for access to the medium. If no traffic is detected on the medium, the station may send a transmission.
CSMA/CD	Carrier Sense Multiple Access with Collision Detection. A characteristic of network hardware that uses CSMA in conjunction with a process that detects when two stations transmit simultaneously. If that happens, both stations back off and retry the transmission after a random period of time has elapsed.
DARPA	Defense Advanced Research Projects Agency. Originally called ARPA. The government agency that funded the research that developed the ARPANET.

Term	*Definition*
Datagram	A packet of data and delivery information.
DHCP	Dynamic Host Configuration Protocol. A protocol that provides dynamic address allocation and automatic TCP/IP configuration.
Digital	A type of communication used by computers, consisting of individual on/off pulses. Compare to analog.
Directed broadcast address	An IP address that specifies all hosts on the network.
Domain	The highest subdivision of the Internet, for the most part by country (except in the U.S., where it's by type of organization, such as educational, commercial, and government). Usually the last part of a host name. For example, the domain part of ibm.com is .com, which represents the domain of commercial sites in the U.S.
Domain Name System (DNS)	The system that translates between Internet IP address and Internet host names.
Ethernet	A type of local area network hardware. Many TCP/IP networks are Ethernet-based.
FDDI	Fiber Distributed Data Interface. The formal name for fiber wiring.
FDM	Frequency Division Multiplexing. A technique of passing signals across a single medium by assigning each signal a unique carrier frequency.
Firewall	A device placed on a network to prevent unauthorized traffic from entering the network.
FQDN	Fully Qualified Domain Name. A combination of the host name and the domain name.

Term	*Definition*
Frame	Packets as transmitted across a medium. Differing frame types have unique characteristics.
Frame relay	A type of digital data communication protocol.
FTP	File Transfer Protocol. A popular Internet communication protocol that allows you to transfer files between hosts on the Internet.
Gateway	A device that interfaces two networks using different protocols.
Hardware address	The physical address of a host used by networks.
Host	A server using TCP/IP and/or that is connected to the Internet.
Host address	A unique number assigned to identify a host on the Internet (also called an IP address or dot address). This address is usually represented as four numbers between 1 and 254 that are separated by periods—for example, 192.58.107.230.
Host ID	The portion of an IP address that identifies the host in a particular network. It is used in conjunction with network IDs to form a complete IP address.
Host name	A unique name for a host that corresponds to the host address.
HTML	Hypertext Markup Language. The formatting language/protocol used to define various text styles in a hypertext document, including emphasis and bulleted lists.
HTTP	Hypertext Transfer Protocol. The communications protocol used by WWW services to retrieve documents quickly.

Term	*Definition*
ICMP	Internet Control Message Protocol. A maintenance protocol that handles error messages to be sent when datagrams are discarded or when systems experience congestion.
IGMP	Internet Group Management Protocol. A protocol used to carry group membership information in a multicast system.
ISDN	Integrated Services Digital Network. A dedicated telephone line connection that transmits digital data at the rate of 64 to 128 Kbps.
LAN	Local Area Network. A network of computers that is usually limited to a small physical area, such as a building.
LLC	Logical Link Control. A protocol that provides a common interface point to the MAC layers.
MAC	Media Access Control. A protocol that governs which access method a station has to the network.
MAN	Metropolitan Area Network. A physical communications network that operates across a metropolitan area.
MIME	Multipurpose Internet Mail Extension. A protocol that describes the format of Internet messages.
Name resolution	The process of mapping a computer name to an IP address. LMHosts and WINS are two ways of resolving names.
NFS	Network File System. A file system developed by Sun Microsystems that is now widely used on many different networks.
NIC	Network Interface Card. An add-on card that lets a machine access a LAN (most commonly an Ethernet card).

Term	*Definition*
Nodes	Individual computers connected to a network.
OSI	Open Systems Interconnection. A set of ISO standards (the current standards for encoding data onto CD-ROMs) that defines the framework for implementing protocols in seven layers.
Packet	The unit of data transmission on the Internet. A packet consists of the data being transferred with additional overhead information, such as the transmitting and receiving addresses.
Packet switching	The communications technology that the Internet is based on, where data being sent between computers is transmitted in packets.
Ping	Packet Internet Groper. A utility that sends a packet to an Internet host and waits for a response. Used to check if a host is up.
POP	Point of Presence. Indicates the availability of a local access number to a public data network.
PPP	Point-to-Point Protocol. A driver that allows you to use a network communications protocol over a phone line. Used with TCP/IP to allow you to have a dial-in Internet host.
PPTP	Point-to-Point Tunneling Protocol. Microsoft's newest protocol to enhance PPP. It offers all the features of PPP, plus security.
Protocol	The standard that defines how computers on a network communicate with one another.
RARP	Reverse Address Resolution Protocol. A protocol that lets a computer find its IP address by broadcasting a request. It is usually used by diskless workstations at startup to find their logical IP addresses.

Term	*Definition*
Repeater	A device that lets you extend the length of your network by amplifying and repeating the information it receives.
RIP	Routing Information Protocol. A router-to-router protocol used to exchange information between routers. RIP supports dynamic routing.
Router	Equipment that receives an Internet packet and sends it to the next machine in the destination path.
Segment	A protocol data unit consisting of part of a stream of bytes being sent between two machines. It also includes information about the current position in the stream and a checksum value.
Server	A provider of a service. A computer that runs services. This term also often refers to a piece of hardware or software that provides access to information requested from it.
Service	An application that processes requests from client applications—for example, storing data or executing an algorithm.
SLIP	Serial Line Internet Protocol. A way of running TCP/IP via phone lines to allow you to have a dialup Internet host.
SMTP	Simple Mail Transport Protocol. The accepted communications protocol standard for the exchange of e-mail between Internet hosts.
SNA	System Network Architecture. A protocol suite developed and used by IBM.
SNMP	Simple Network Management Protocol. A communications protocol used to control and monitor devices on a network.

Term	*Definition*
Socket	A means of network communication via special entities.
Subnet	Any lower network that is part of the logical network. Identified by the network ID.
Subnet mask	A 32-bit value that distinguishes the network ID from the host ID in an IP address.
TCP/IP	Transmission Control Protocol/Internet Protocol. A communications protocol suite that allows computers of any make to communicate when running TCP/IP software.
TFTP	Trivial File Transfer Protocol. A basic, standard protocol used to upload or download files with minimal overhead. TFTP depends on UDP and is often used to initialize diskless workstations, because it has no directory or password capabilities.
Transceiver	A device that connects a host interface to a network. It is used to apply signals to the cable and to sense collisions.
UDP	User Datagram Protocol. A simple protocol that lets an application program on one machine send a datagram to an application program on another machine. Delivery is not guaranteed, nor is it guaranteed that the datagrams will be delivered in the proper order.
URL	Uniform Resource Locator. A means of specifying the location of information on the Internet for WWW clients.
WAN	Wide Area Network. A network of computers that are geographically dispersed.
X.25	A CCITT standard for connecting computers to a network that provides a reliable stream

Term	Definition
	transmission service that can support remote logins.
X.400	A CCITT standard for message transfer and interpersonal messaging, such as electronic mail.

Additional Terms and Concepts

_____

_____

_____

_____

_____

_____

_____

_____

_____

_____

_____

_____

_____

_____

_____

_____

_____

_____

_____

Not every interesting item the instructor has to share with the class is neccesarily related directly to the exam. That's the case with "Did You Know?" Think of the information in here as the intriguing sidebar, or the interesting diversion, you might wish the instructor would share with you during an aside.

CHAPTER 9

Did You Know?

The following are interesting items not relevant to the exam:

- The price of 100 MB Ethernet technology is dropping almost daily. Most vendors make hubs that can switch between 10MB and 100MB. It is highly recommended that, if you are dedicated to Ethernet, all new hubs you purchase be switchable, for there will be a time in the near future when 10MB will be only a memory.

- Although IPCONFIG is the tool to use on NT networks to see your TCP/IP configuration information, WINIPCFG (undocumented in the manuals) is the tool to use in Windows 95. Offering the same information, it is Windows-based in nature, easier to use, and simple enough for a user to understand. A version of it for Windows NT can be found in the Windows NT Resource Kit.

- The Registry, in addition to being the heart of the operating system for all current flavors of Windows, also holds networking configuration information. Here you can change values directly for many things in Windows NT, including the following:

The name of the computer	HKEY_LOCAL_MACHINE\SYSTEM\CurrentControlSet\Control\ComputerName\ActiveComputerName\ComputerName
Adapter description	HKEY_LOCAL_MACHINE\SOFTWARE\Microsoft\Windows NT\CurrentVersion\NetworkCards\1\Description
Adapter manufacturer	HKEY_LOCAL_MACHINE\SOFTWARE\Microsoft\Windows NT\CurrentVersion\NetworkCards\1\Manufacturer
Default domain at logon prompt	HKEY_LOCAL_MACHINE\SOFTWARE\Microsoft\Windows NT\CurrentVersion\Winlogon\DefaultDomainName

Logon banner   HKEY_LOCAL_
                                          MACHINE\SOFTWARE\
                                          Microsoft\Windows
                                          NT\CurrentVersion\Winlogo
                                          n\LegalNoticeCaption and
                                          HKEY_LOCAL_
                                          MACHINE\SOFTWARE\
                                          Microsoft\Windows
                                          NT\CurrentVersion\Winlogo
                                          n\LegalNoticeText

INDEX

R

radio transmission, 51
  local area networks (LANs), 75
RAID (Redundant Array of Inexpensive Disks), fault tolerance, 142-143
ranking questions, 233-234
RARP (Reverse Address Resolution Protocol), 262
RAS (Remote Access Service), 212-213
  troubleshooting, 177
    authentication, 178
    AutoDial at logon, 178
    Callback with Multilink, 178
Read share permission, 136
Redundant Array of Inexpensive Disks (RAID), fault tolerance, 142-143
Registry, 268
Remote Access Service, *see* RAS
remote monitoring (Performance Monitor), 154
repeaters, 30-31, 252, 263
Report view (Performance Monitor), 151
Replicator group, 128
Reverse Address Resolution Protocol, *see* RARP
Ring topologies, 88
RISC boot sequence, troubleshooting, 171
routers, 33-36, 263
  brouters, 258
  RIP, 36, 283
  routing tables, global versus local, 35-36

S

sample questions, 241-249
satellite microwave systems, 80
/scsiordinal switch (BOOT.INI), 175
searching for events (Event Viewer), 163
security
  accounts
    auditing changes, 130-131
    system policies, 129, 131-134
  disk resources, 135
    NTFS permissions, 137-139
    share permissions, 135-136
  share-level, 17
  user-level, 18
Security log, 160
segments, 263
Serial Line Internet Protocol (SLIP), 39, 263
Server object counters (Performance Monitor), 153-154
servers, 18-19, 263
  server-based networking, 18
services, 263
Services load phase, troubleshooting, 175
Session layer (OSI model), 28, 251
Session Stats pane (Network Monitor), 165
share permissions, 135-136
  combining with NTFS permissions, 139
share-level security, 17
shielded twisted-pair (STP) cable, 65
  attenuation, 66
  capacity of, 66

WE WANT TO KNOW WHAT YOU THINK

To better serve you, we would like your opinion on the content and quality of this book. Please complete this card and mail it to us or fax it to 317-581-4663.

Name _____

Address _____

City _____ State_____ Zip _____

Phone _____ Email Address _____

Occupation _____

Which certification exams have you already passed? _____
_____
_____
_____

Which certification exams do you plan to take? __
_____
_____
_____

What influenced your purchase of this book?
❑ Recommendation   ❑ Cover Design
❑ Table of Contents   ❑ Index
❑ Magazine Review   ❑ Advertisement
❑ Publisher's reputation ❑ Author Name

How would you rate the contents of this book?
❑ Excellent   ❑ Very Good
❑ Good   ❑ Fair
❑ Below Average   ❑ Poor

What other types of certification products will you buy/have you bought to help you prepare for the exam?
❑ Quick reference books ❑ Testing software
❑ Study guides   ❑ Other

What do you like most about this book? Check all that apply.
❑ Content   ❑ Writing Style
❑ Accuracy   ❑ Examples
❑ Listings   ❑ Design
❑ Index   ❑ Page Count
❑ Price   ❑ Illustrations

What do you like least about this book? Check all that apply.
❑ Content   ❑ Writing Style
❑ Accuracy   ❑ Examples
❑ Listings   ❑ Design
❑ Index   ❑ Page Count
❑ Price   ❑ Illustrations

What would be a useful follow-up book to this one for you?_____
Where did you purchase this book?_____
Can you name a similar book that you like better than this one, or one that is as good? Why?_____
_____

How many New Riders books do you own? _____
What are your favorite certification or general computer book titles? _____
_____

What other titles would you like to see us develop? _____
_____

Any comments for us? _____
_____

Fold here and Scotch tape to mail

New Riders
201 W. 103rd St.
Indianapolis, IN 46290